Memoirs of a Sex Slave Survivor

Written by Timea Nagy

This book is dedicated to Michael Josifovic, and Mario Catenaccio, as well as law enforcement officers around the world who work tirelessly to protect sex trafficking victims and to my fellow sex trafficking survivors.

Forward

Digging through a trash dumpster looking for used condoms in the wee hours of the morning was not exactly what a young and dedicated law enforcement agent had bargained for when he raised his right hand and swore to protect the Constitution as a Special Agent with the Federal Bureau of Investigation.

An Overland Park, Kansas Police Department Detective probably thought he would be spending his work hours arresting burglars and car thieves, not discreetly following young Asian woman upon their arrival at the Kansas City airport as they were transported to local massage parlors.

However unusual or repulsive the job, it was the tenacious work of these two dedicated law enforcement officers and many others, over a long period of time, that brought an end to a residential prostitution ring bearing all the hallmarks of human trafficking.

The day of the raids in the human trafficking investigation was May 10, 2007, a Thursday. Scores of federal agents and police executed search warrants in sixteen locations in the Kansas City suburbs. Coincidentally, Thursday is the day that Kansas City's alternative free newspaper, Pitch Weekly hit the streets in various locations around the Kansas City metropolitan area, with its nearly two million residents.

As law enforcement officers escorted scores of Asian women from the massage parlors to shelters throughout the area, dozens of newly printed advertisements in the Pitch promoted, "oriental massage", "table shower", "body shampoo", and other services offered at the businesses from early morning until late evening. The ads disappeared soon after the FBI raids.

While the investigations into the activity at the massage parlors in the Kansas City suburbs was categorized by the FBI as a human trafficking investigation, in fact, federal prosecutors did not believe that they could prove the elements of that crime beyond a reasonable doubt. Instead, they charged the owners of the massage parlors with various other federal violations related to prostitution and movement of women across state and international borders for the purposes of prostitution.

The conditions that lead to this investigation are far from unique in North America. Across the United States and Canada, in most major cities and many smaller metropolitan areas, scores of sex servicing establishments, including massage parlors and topless nightclubs, operate as legal and sanctioned businesses. In many of the businesses, behind the scenes, unknown to most of the aloof or uncaring customers, exists human trafficking.

Human trafficking is the process by which human beings are placed in conditions of slavery. Human trafficking is recruiting, harboring, transporting, placing or using individuals in jobs for little or no pay. It is modern day slavery. It is not something that *resembles* slavery as some have called it. Human trafficking *is* slavery. And it exists in every country in the world. It exists in the prostitution industry, in domestic and commercial cleaning services, farm and factory labor and many more.

One might think that this is improbable, even impossible, given that slavery is outlawed in every country in the world. But it exists today in a far greater magnitude than it ever existed in history. In fact, more human beings are being held as slaves at this moment than ever came to the United States during the entire 350 year history of African slave trade.

The United States Department of State estimates that there are over 15,000 new victims trafficked into the United States every year who become slaves in one job description or another. To most casual observers, this is very perplexing, since slavery has been outlawed in the United States since the passage of the Thirteenth Amendment to the United States Constitution on January 31, 1865. Most Americans are unaware of the extent or even the existence of this gross injustice. For all intents and purposes, it is an unseen, unheard and unreported crime. But it exists, in many cases, in plain sight, generating three billion dollars in profit for the slave holders.

The bondage of today's slavery is perpetuated by isolation, threats and coercion and in some cases, physical violence. Its list of victims does not discriminate on the basis of sex, age or ethnic origin. Human beings, from all corners of the globe, young and old, are slaves in every country in the world.

I got my first close-up view of human trafficking, in all its depravity, as an FBI Special Agent in Kansas City. The Kansas City field office, one of fifty-six field FBI divisions throughout the United States, has jurisdictional responsibility for the entire state of Kansas and about two thirds of Missouri. Human trafficking cases started to appear on the Kansas City FBI radar in about 2004.

In that year the FBI investigated the case of Arlan and Linda Kaufman, who contracted with the state of Kansas to house the mentally ill in group homes that they operated. Instead of caring for the patients, they forced them to work naked on their farm. To add insult to injury, they forced the victims to perform various sex acts on one another while being videotaped.

In 2006, the Kansas City FBI investigated the case of Russian youths being forced to work driving an ice cream truck up to 14 hours a day, at the grand total hourly wage of 87 cents per hour.

It was also in 2006 that the Overland Park, Kansas City Police Department began an investigation, joined by the FBI, which resulted in the raids on 16 locations associated with an Asian massage parlor and prostitution ring that was operating in the Kansas City suburbs.

One case, involving Asian massage parlors, became a focus of the FBI and police. It was code named "China Rose" because that was the name of one of the strip center massage parlors under investigation. This case involved the most participants, including the masseuses themselves, most of whom were considered by the FBI to be potential victims of human trafficking.

In fact, of all the human trafficking cases investigated on a nationwide basis by the FBI, about fifty percent involve the commercial sex industry, including massage parlors, brothels and strip clubs.

There is at least one thing that the owners of these establishments know about their customers: they come for sex and they are willing to pay for it. There is a seemingly unending demand for sexual services provided by these establishments. Their owners are more than willing to provide the supply to meet the demand. However, in order to do that, the owners must find a supply of young and attractive woman who are able and willing to go to work to meet the demand and generate profits for the establishment owners. One major problem is that many women who work in these places may be young and able, but are not willing.

In the cases where the women are not willing, in which they are being coerced to work under threat, intimidation or actual violence, we have human trafficking. These women are being held as slaves and forced to work as prostitutes. Most, if not all of their revenue, is taken by their captors, the establishment owners.

The trafficked women, arriving in the Unites States and Canada come in most cases from China, Mexico and Europe. The circumstances of their transition into human trafficking vary considerably. Some are lured by false marriage proposals and some are kidnapped. Other victims are sold by boyfriends, family members and even parents. In some cases, the victims have answered advertisements that have lured them with promises of legitimate jobs as nannies, babysitters or restaurant hostesses. It was this method that was used to make the author of this book, Timea Nagy, a sex slave.

I first met Timea in New York City at an event that was unrelated to human trafficking. I told her about my background as an FBI agent and she told me about her past as a human trafficking victim. The story she told me is a prime example of the process and nature of human trafficking. In the sex industry, there are an untold number of victims that have had or will have the same thing happen to them that happened to Timea.

Timea's story is important because it is a first-hand account of the circumstances that lead to enslavement. It illustrates the power the traffickers have over the victims by showing what was going on in her mind that affected her decisions during the crucial time that she was becoming a victim. Her story illustrates the exact nature by which human trafficking victims, to satisfy the greed and profit motives of their owners, are tricked, coerced and manipulated. What happened to Timea is how the traffickers work. Unless they are stopped, they will continue to victimize young women and in the process, destroy lives.

By the time I had met Timea, she had already decided that she had kept her story secret for too long. It was time to let the world know what had happened. The time had come to raise public awareness, train police officers, educate lawmakers, and most importantly, warn other young women who might experience the same circumstances as Timea, before they become victims.

There has been much written about human trafficking, but Timea's story is told from the eyes of the victim, a sex slave survivor. It makes an important contribution to the study and prevention of this despicable crime. It is our hope that it opens the eyes of the public and helps to eradicate human slavery.

Jeff Lanza
Retired FBI Agent

Introduction

Writing this book has been extremely difficult. Completing it was one of the most difficult things I've ever done in my life. Now that it's complete, I am proud to be able to share my truth. I'm proud to be able to inspire, support, and educate anyone touched by my story. This book is not for the faint of heart. My story is real and it is raw. Nevertheless, the person who emerged from the horrific experiences you'll soon read about is a strong and determined woman; a woman who is ready to help those around her and to work to prevent these things from happening again.

So how does a person survive sex slavery, rape, and blackmail? There is no guide. All I know is that it has taken me ten years to get to where I am today. I am now prepared to tell my story. And it will be worth it. I began doing seminars in 2009 and quickly realized the effect that my story had on others. I've educated hundreds of front-line workers. And I have helped and supported many survivors of the same crimes I've faced. These people are the inspiration for this book.

By sharing my story I am exposing a truth. A truth about myself and a truth about the world we all live in. This book describes my emotional journey over the last decade. For my protection and the protection of others I have occasionally altered personal details herein. Please know that I have stayed true to the substance of my story.

While I recognize that it is important for me to tell my story as truthfully as possible, there are details which I have omitted from this story which I do not feel comfortable sharing as yet. The substance of my story is not impacted by these omissions, but these very personal details relate to information and experiences which I am still processing. If anything, they relate to a possible second edition or continuation of this story that may evolve in time.

A Note on the Title - Sex Trade Survivor, not victim

My life hasn't been easy. I was raised in poverty by an alcoholic father. My teenage years were tough. I've faced death, rape, abuse, and survived sex slavery and human trafficking. But I'm still here. I'm still standing. In fact, I'm smiling. That's right, I am smiling. As you begin to read my story, it is important to remember that my experiences have made me stronger because I have survived them. I have steadfastly refused to succumb to the cult of victimization which can engulf people who have come through what I have come through. I challenge my readers, the people I help, the professionals I educate and the network that supports me to do the same.

Everyone has a story. You may be reading this book because something difficult happened to you when you were a child, teenager, or young adult. Something challenging may have happened to you recently, or to someone you know and love. Either way, I hope you're here because you want to get on with your life and move beyond your circumstances.

If you do fall into the categories above, then you may be shocked or relieved to hear this fact:

You are not a Victim. You are a Survivor.

If you think of yourself as a victim, then you'll continue to be a victim for the rest of your life. Unconsciously you'll create different situations over and over again to prove it to yourself. There may be different settings, different players, but the end result will be the same. You'll continually re-victimize yourself by framing yourself as a victim, and creating life circumstances that enable victimhood.

Over the past several years, I've learned a lot about people and their stories. I've learned that things are never as simple as they seem. Because of that, I've learned the valuable lesson of never judging a situation precipitously. The bus driver who is in a terrible mood may have just found out that his wife has breast cancer. The guy you think doesn't have a care in the world driving his shiny new BMW might have a son on the battlefields of Iraq who he hasn't heard from in four months. The lady standing in line at the bank in front of you who just screamed at the teller saying she has three kids at home to feed when the bank just took her last $26 in late fees.

Each of these stories is true. I know this because I spoke to each of these people. It took me about three to five minutes, but their truths were revealed.

We all have a story. We all have challenges and obstacles. Our choices are manifested through the way we handle life's difficulties. Do we choose to remain victims and use our circumstances as excuses to opt out through drugs, alcohol, food and shopping? Or, do we see these challenges as opportunities to learn something about ourselves, let go of limiting beliefs and thoughts and live our best lives possible?

Terrible things happen all the time - just read a newspaper if you don't believe me. But, life goes on -

spring always follows winter. Dawn always follows even the darkest night. Time marches on, and your life will go on. There will always be new challenges to which you can succumb as a victim, or you can stand up, advocate for yourself, and become a survivor. In my counseling and outreach work I enable survivors. This book describes the experiences, journey and choices which contributed to making me the survivor I am today.

Chapter 1

1998, April 18th

I was sitting on a Toronto bound airplane next to an older Hungarian woman. I was bursting with excitement and enthusiasm about my upcoming Canadian adventure and I could not wait to get airborne and start my journey. My travel-mate, in a friendly and conversational tone, asked "Do you speak any English?"

I shook my head negatively and explained that the woman who approached me from the agency had said English wasn't mandatory for the au pair role she had lined up for me. I'd be able to learn another language and experience the world from a broader scope; one unknown to my grandparents and great grandparents before them. Her eyes didn't echo the effervescent excitement mine expressed, but I didn't care. Maybe she hadn't seen the same movies I had - I was excited!

In a slightly more concerned tone, she asked "What exactly will you be doing there?"

"Babysitting or cleaning," I replied matter of factly. "Whatever the job is, I'm prepared for it."

She looked at me skeptically, and asked. "You weren't told your specific duties?"

I regurgitated a version of what I remembered. "I'm to be briefed when I arrive. The agency arranged for me to be met as soon as I get off the tarmac and from there we will make our way to my accommodation."

"Which is… where exactly?" She asked, this time barely masking her disbelief and concern with my obvious naiveté.

"I don't have the address, exactly, but I'm sure it'll be nicer then my place in Hungary. It's only a three month stay - maybe a nice hotel?"

I smiled at her, hoping she would stop asking questions and just let me stare into the sea below, which she did, but not without first insisting I take her card. I put it in my wallet and turned my back to her, laid the top of my head against the cool window and got a deeper view of Holland below.

As we bustled off the plane, I felt like an American actress. Hollywood was everywhere, even in this Canadian airport. Acres of white teeth were always smiling; waving stewardesses directed me on my way and brazen teenage boys teased each other in casual spoken English that I'd never heard before. Pinball machine like toilets flushed themselves and people laughed loudly with hair that seemed to bounce like fine grass.

Approaching customs, I saw uniformed guards looking people in the eye. They drank from paper coffee cups which I'd only seen in movies before and I had to stop myself from staring at them. I hadn't even left the airport and I already felt like a newborn baby watching bustling rush hour commotion, amazed and baffled by the strange new world before me.

In order to get my work permit, I still had some hoops to jump through. Pressing on past the candy machines, I found my way to customs, handed in my paper work and waited for my employment permit. The female officer asked me a few questions in English and I didn't understand a word of what she said. She said the same series of questions again, slower, louder and more suspiciously. When I clearly couldn't understand her, she pointed to a chair and I sat down in it. After four hours, the translator showed up. He relayed question after question and then translated my Hungarian answers back into English for the agent. He told me she was suspicious because my paper work indicated that I was to be a dancer in an exotic club, and that I would be paying my Canadian agent $140 a week. They told me my story didn't match the contract I signed with the agency in Hungary and because of this discrepancy they had no choice but to send me home, however this interview had lasted for 8 hours and I'd missed the last plane out.

"The men responsible for your contract are outside," the translator said. "They'll have you back here for your flight to Hungary at 3 P.M. tomorrow."

I left the immigration office and walked straight into the arms of two Hungarian men, confused and tired. They both look pissed and I asked them who they were. It turned out that one of them was a Hungarian ex-cop. My mother had spent her working life as a police officer in Hungary but was now retired and this man immediately knew who she was. 'That's a good sign,' I thought optimistically.

Outside the arrivals area a large SUV was waiting. Inside, I was happy to finally hear someone speaking my own language. Even with a head muddy and confused from travel, I tried to make light conversation as we pulled off into the night, but it was clear they were angry. I had no idea where we were going and they spoke exclusively to each other.

We sped past automobiles of all shapes and sizes on the eight lane highway. My thoughts danced around irrationally and I couldn't tell if I was leading them or they were leading me and I began to feel more and more vulnerable as unfamiliar buildings sprung up around us. Skyscrapers, all of them, they stood enviably close to the stars while I lost my battle with sleep and drifted off into an exhausted but anxious slumber.

At a two story motel with paint peeling off its walls, I followed the two men up a narrow staircase to the top floor. Entering what I supposed would be my room for the night; I took my shoes off and tentatively felt the deep red carpet under my toes. It stank like stale extinguished cigarettes. I was growing increasingly apprehensive, lost in my new surroundings, exhausted and confused. My "agency representatives" finally spoke to me, in Hungarian. Two young, soft-spoken, clean cut men who would have looked more believable as bank tellers as opposed to the human traffickers they turned out to be.

"You'll have a lawyer fighting for you to stay with us and he won't be cheap. The men in this country hold doctorate degrees in law and charge by the hour. So you must become comfortable inside our pockets for awhile. In order to see some light again, you'll be dancing. It's the fastest way to make money and in your best interest. You'll also tell immigration you'll be dancing when we return to the airport tomorrow."

They looked at one another, then me. "I'm not a dancer. The woman at the agency told me I could baby-sit and clean houses…"

"Well, the longer our stay is tomorrow at immigration, the more you'll owe us for the lawyer. So convince them quick. Arouse them with wit if you need to, but remember: the longer we stay, the longer you dance, dancer."

Flashing traces of a smile, the original brown eyed man (who really could have been your third grade teacher) spoke up once more. "Wasn't your mother a police officer? They know my family, I thought. "Yes, yes with some bits of white hair in her bangs. And your brother, her lovely son Josef! They all have a very particular way they do everything, your kin. I could always pick them out in a crowd." They know my family. The implied threat was clear.

Without sleeping, we got up off the bed and continued back into the night. We were off to the club where I'd be working.

You see, it doesn't happen the way people imagine it does. They don't chain you to the bed. They didn't lock me in any bathroom. They forced my participation using coercion and intimidation. I couldn't be responsible for the murder of my family by not co-operating with the Hungarian mafia. I was only nineteen years old.

I finished another cup of hotel coffee near a subdivision and a shopping center. We drove just past the lights of the big box stores and their empty parking lots and arrived at my workplace. The lights were flashing brightly as I entered, and hurt my eyes. I walked into a hustling and bustling strip joint during its busiest hour.

Near the front of the action, "pervert's row" was populated with eager men in sunglasses veiling eyes that flicked with reptilian rapidity from the stage to each other and back to the stage again. It was dark, but I could see what was happening. I quickly and quietly went into shock as the two chauffeurs watched me watch the scene before me. My body went numb and the girl who had boarded a plane in Budapest twenty-four hours ago slowly disappeared.

The owner of the club was the Canadian agent my Hungarian contact told me about. I was never meant to clean or baby-sit. I was a recruited stripper and couldn't leave or my family would die.

Alfonso, the owner, took me downstairs to a dressing room and showed me a rack of clothes – dancing clothes – provocative, skimpy and suggestive. He pointed to a tacky shoe collection against the opposite wall. He waited until I chose a dress and shoes and then pointed to his desk, instructing me to sit on it. I did as I was told, but I didn't take my eyes off him for a second. He spread my legs and pulled up my skirt. He was sweating, but strangely calm as if this was just part of his daily routine. I felt pain, but kept my focus on him, looking for any trace of humanity inside his eyes - desperate to assert myself in some way.

He was a big man, soft spoken and quiet, but really big. As he was "checking the new horse - inside and out," his breathing got faster and faster until finally he stopped. When he finished, he got up, smacked my behind, and then walked me out of his office to the stage area. My legs and hands were shaking nervously. I felt belittled, tricked and vulnerable. It was one of the most humiliating experiences of my entire life. I wondered what my new price tag was. Sitting down at a table, the chauffeurs looked at me. My insides hurt from the damage caused by the owner's unshorn nails.

"He likes you, you know."

I didn't look up as I struggled to regain my composure.

"He doesn't like everyone who comes in here, so consider yourself lucky."

I felt myself bleeding.

"Don't you want him to take you shopping sometime?" They asked. "He wants you to look your best out there, don't you see?"

Sitting, shivering from the cold and with my matted hair draped over the front of my face, I couldn't believe that this was actually happening. I thought for a moment that I might be having a nightmare that would end when I woke up. As I looked up at the men across from me I began to understand that I wouldn't escape them by waking up. The damage done by the owner's long nails would have woken me up from even the deepest nightmare. This was my new reality.

Another Eastern European girl was instructed to sit beside me at our table. She was instructed to show me the ropes (or poles, as it were) but my limbs were numb and useless. I hadn't slept in over a day and had been intermittently fed weak coffee and strong trauma since I had stepped off the plane. Shock and exhaustion were beginning to take their toll.

The clientele had been shown out for the night by the bouncer and I could sense the sun coming up outside. The girl, Alexandra, got on stage. With a mix of false confidence and well intentioned traipsing, she did two catwalk laps around in her high heels. "Your turn," She said glibly, smiling shallow eyes at me.

The owner and my two chauffeurs were dimly outlined by the light streaming in through the front door. They didn't talk to one another with what seemed like false confidence, they smoked cigarettes while I learned. Long into the morning I followed her movements. Alexandra's instructions were robotic and spoken without insistence - she had no home to hurry back to.

Alexandra said that I must use a towel when sitting on a client in VIP and gave me tips on how to spot men that would try to bite me. The owner chimed in something about 'damaged goods.'

I just wanted to fall asleep and wake up in my little bed in my little room with my cat right next to me, to the sound of my brother yelling because, once again, I hadn't taken out the garbage.

Chapter 2

The now familiar motel room smell comprised of generic cleanser and instant coffee odor greeted me when I woke up. My eyelids quickly, albeit reluctantly, batted open and the same two Hungarian guys came in with the club owner, Alfonzo, in tow. The three 'men' smoked inside the room and looked at me while they inhaled deeply. "Well, the good news is you're going home. But the better news for you is that it's not for long, seeing you still owe us a steadily increasing fee for the expenses you've incurred, and of course we would like to help you to make the money for your house that you owe. See, we are here to help you."

"Your flight," the chauffeur continued undeterred, "leaves at four today. That's two hours from now. It will be a flight occupied, unbeknownst to you, with people watching you. Just to make sure you get home safe, of course."

"Do you understand?" he asked.

On the plane home I couldn't stop formulating and comparing the different variables and possible outcomes of the most colorful escape plans conceivable. I was left, again, with no options. I could be responsible for the deaths of my immediate family and live forever on the lam or I could dance to pay off debt under a pseudonym in a place where no one knew who I was. Anyone who questions my motives, or the motives of any woman placed in this impossible position, does so with ignorance of a woman's protective instincts towards her family.

As soon as I got home and deplaned, my cell phone rang. It was the female voice from the agency. When I first met her she was not nearly this focused or instructive. She said that she would be coming to my house and that I would need to give her a passport photo immediately.

All I wanted to say to her was "You failed to mention anything to me about having my insides inspected by perverts who wouldn't let me sleep when we first met." But, resigned to my fate, I didn't. The line remained silent.

"What did you say?" my employment agent asked.

"Nothing." I responded, coldly, and I hung up - shaking from a combination of exhaustion and disgust.

Within a week she came to my apartment with my new passport, new name and work papers. She told me that there would once again be unknown observers on my flight back to Toronto.

Before the end of the week, I was on a plane with a new name, fake age and a fictitious identity. I knew this was illegal but I was so busy looking over my shoulder trying to figure out who was following me that I never bothered to try to signal the authorities. I knew that there was no way out of this and cried in the airplane bathroom for the majority of the flight to Toronto's Pearson Airport. I remembered that woman who sat next to me on my first trip, her words repeating in my mind endlessly as I closed my eyes.

"If I get through this," I thought, "I will never leave home again. I will steel my nerves and just pay the money I 'owe' and go home in three months; that's it."

I landed in Toronto, again.

The contrast between this experience and my last arrival was glaring. Stranger's conversations and headlines glared obtrusively at me, seeming sinister for the first time. Either I had been renovated, or this airport had been. It seemed that so much had changed, but perhaps it was only the loss of my initial excitement. The feeling of wanting to jump out of my skin with excitement about my imminent discovery of a new land had faded away and I wondered if this is what death in a retirement home felt like. During the long slow stroll back to the chauffeurs I felt like a prisoner bereft of hope, who had aged mentally beyond her years.

I walked off the plane towards Customs. I had my fake passport and my new work permit. I didn't know if I was more afraid of getting caught with the fake passport and going to jail or getting through immigration and facing what lurked beyond airport security.

"You're here to dance?"

I nodded affirmatively.

"You understand dance? The verb, 'to dance?' You're a dancer in Hungary are you?"

I nodded again.

The weight of his stamp thudded, and with the sound, he issued me a Canadian work permit. I felt like I was going to vomit onto the glass barrier separating us because, deep inside I'd been harboring hopes that I would get caught and sent home.

I walked towards the exit and wasn't surprised when I saw my coercers again. These two men were some of the most notorious traffickers of Hungarian women in Canada, but they behaved as if they were simply going to work and doing a job they were good at like anyone else. Their ability to normalize their objectifying behavior and to matter of factly enforce collusion from the girls never ceased to amaze me.

We headed out of the airport. The highway was mid-day rush hour busy and we got stuck in traffic. I smiled at a child in the car next to us who immediately ducked his blushing head between his legs and thrust up two tiny fingers. It was the sign of peace for me to see while his head stayed hidden.

"You did the right thing by coming back." The driving chauffeur said. "That was very smart of you. The next three months will fly by - just think, before you know it you'll be home again with your family and you will pay off all of your debts. And your house will be paid for. It's okay, you're in good hands. We're like a family here. I know you've never danced before but you will pick it up quickly, the other girls will help you."

The traffic began lurching forward again and we were on our way to the same derelict motel I'd been billeted in before. We walked into the old motel room and it felt as though all the time that had passed since I'd left disappeared, negated from existence.

On the wall above my single bed hung reprinted paintings of people in fields that somehow had coffee stains in all four corners. The bathroom still smelled like bleach and the off-white sheets stuck to my calves.

My chauffeurs told me to take a shower and get ready because Alfonzo was waiting, so I did as I was told. After torturing myself in front of the mirror for a moment about events that were sure to come, I sat beside the window, despondently. The men tied their shoes as I looked outside.

I saw a huge highway and a shopping mall branded with colorful and child-friendly letters. Ironically it read "Toy's 'R' Us". I read it over and over and over again, trying to figure it out what it meant. We are toys. Toys are we, play with us… My mind was racing.

Could I fake 'sexy' long enough to earn my way out of this? What if I didn't convince the men at the club? What would become of me and my family if I was physically, mentally and emotionally unable to strip for money? I had scarcely been naked in front of my boyfriend and we had been an item for two years. I was just a girl, slowly learning what it meant to be a woman as we made our way back to the sour aesthetic and glaring lights of the strip club.

Chapter 3

In my first few days I got acquainted with the other eighty girls the club employed. Mostly eastern European, we were divided into groups of six. All of us worked for Alfonzo but not all of us danced. Many were professional prostitutes who walked the streets or were driven around town by other chauffeurs disguised as taxi drivers. Perhaps this was what happened to girls who couldn't handle the spotlights of the club? Threats, implicit and explicit were everywhere in this environment.

Ukrainians, Hungarians, Romanians and Bulgarians came in and out of the club routinely, but I never saw one try to escape. It was all I could think of, but, as if I was telepathically linked to my captors, whenever these thoughts surfaced I would 'overhear' cautionary violent nightmares designed to discourage these thoughts.

"So I just got off the phone with Sasha in Ukraine, you know Sasha. Yeah, exactly. Insane Sasha. Well he was bringing forty girls from Hungary to fly out of Frankfurt when one of them got brave."

"Did he take care of it?"

"Well, yeah," the chauffeur laughed like a cartoon. "Remember how he had that old baseball bat he never washed off? He fucking cleaned her clock until springs sprung out her ears and left her mangled by some German farmhouse's garbage cab and he couldn't say if she made it or not." He laughed again. "Hell, we all make choices right?"

"Man, good thing we don't have issues of that kind in this camp."

I don't have to tell you how quickly I stopped thinking about running away. I never even spoke to the other girls. We ate in the club together, we showered in the club together, but we didn't speak. Canada's fabled natural majesty was quickly reduced to a five minute drive between the club and my germ infested motel room.

This beautiful country became a house of submission. I was forced to dance for any man who called me, I danced for men who were penniless, senile, lacking in hygiene and/or restraint. To these men I was only a plastic robot of objectified entertainment. Needless to say, I wasn't making much money.

One night the bolder of my two chauffeurs surprised me with a visit. He said that he saw me turning clients away, and that I should really start to make money soon. Didn't I know I wasn't a princess? He said I should stop acting like one. I was supposed to make about $400 - $500 a day for them. So on the top of plane ticket and the motel room at this point I owed them an additional $3500.

"So at the rate you're going now, princess, it looks like three months may not be enough." As he finished his sentence, he got up and left the room like a man with something on the stove. The rapidly shifting numbers and figures became a blur as the door to my room opened softly and the Italian shoes and dark pleated suit pants of Alfonzo sauntered in.

"Hello." The club owner said. "Stay."

I started to sweat profusely and didn't know what to do with my hands. He started to talk to me softly but I didn't understand what he was saying. Not once did we make eye contact as he furtively made his way to my bedside. The lamp on the nightstand showed a stain on his Nautica shirt and fingerprints on the cheap belt buckle he was loosening.

I knew there was no way to get out of this, so I initiated, for the first time, the process of transcendence. I left my body. I told myself that I was somewhere else and no matter what happened, that it was only happening to my body. As long as I was compliant, I wouldn't get hurt, and I would survive. The only thing I could do in defense was turn away so that I wouldn't have to see his face or feel his pungent drops of sweat falling on my face.

I was looking at the wall beside me, conjuring happy memories from my childhood - finding bugs and laughing with my brother as we played in the warm afternoon sunlight. I felt him climb on top of me. His belt jabbed at me and his sweat stung when it penetrated my closed eyelids. He was really big and for a moment, I couldn't catch my breath. I gave him a signal and he quickly got off, continuing to touch my lips, breasts and ass through my clothes.

As he began to clumsily undress me, I looked him in the eye and sized him up. He was a middle aged man with hardly any hair left on the top of his head and a tiny pony tail in the back. His eyes were simultaneously dead and predatorily wild. I searched for a human being but found only a ravenous corpse where some light of human warmth should have shone. He was a starving lion. It felt like he had been stalking me his whole life and had just found me: numb, helpless and weak in the legs. And then his pager went off as he was sliding out of his pants.

Hopping up to make a phone call outside, he mimed that he was leaving but would be back to visit again soon. He tried to communicate with me so that I understood, but I was still too far away from my body to fathom any of what just happened.

A second after the owner left, my now familiar chauffeur popped his head in. "So how was he? And how are you?" I stared at him, and I couldn't say anything.

"You're not too tired I see, and almost eager! That must be where the newfound popularity comes from." There was a knock on the door. "Oh!" he said, "Some one would like to say hello to you."

He left and another guy came in who looked familiar. As he dropped his keys on the floor, I recalled that he was the main driver for the club. A driver who was also a soft-spoken man, he bumbled over small talk and dropped his wallet before undressing me and kissing the outside of my mouth. He was soft, he was gentle, but I had no control. He had sex with me, while I was looking at the top of the ceiling, entering me over and over again. No it did not hurt physically, no he did not smell, or look like mafia He didn't hit me, or hurt me. He had sex with me without my consent and against my will. He entered me over and over again. I wasn't in pain physically, I was in pain emotionally.

He looked at my naked body while he was on top of me. I felt dirty. I was scared. I felt like my whole body was being covered by invisible dirt that would not be easy to wash away. I thought about my boyfriend. Would he be mad at me if he knew? Was this rape? Was I cheating? All I knew was that it was nothing like the movies I'd seen. I wanted to scream…but really…I had no "reason" to. He wasn't hurting me, well not physically at least.

As soon as he left, I went to the bathroom to cleanse myself. I looked at my body, saw all the hand prints on my legs, breasts and neck and I started to wash myself. I grabbed a cheap, rough motel towel and scrubbed myself severely under a sputtering shower head with a bar of soap. I felt as though the shower was ineffective, so I scrubbed harder and harder still. I stopped. The bar of soap had entered the skin breaks that I had just caused by scrubbing myself roughly in order to obliterate any trace of the club owner or the driver. Or, had the men scratched me? Who had hurt my body?

Now that I had been 'trained' by servicing a strange man, the chauffeurs were convinced that I could do more than rack up motel and food bills. I was taken back to the club for another two weeks and as it happened I did start to make money. Of course, it wasn't nearly enough for them and as the days went by I fell deeper and deeper into debt.

Everyday something would be added to my growing tab. "Late for work" - another ten dollars. According to them, until I was out of debt, I was spending 'their' money…I remember, during my second day "on the job" I dared to buy myself a grilled cheese sandwich from the money I'd made. It was the most delicious sandwich I'd ever had. I never knew that a simple slice of cheese on grilled bread could taste so good. At the end of the day when it was time to "cash out," they realized that I had both a ten and five dollar bill. This caught the attention of my handlers because we were normally paid twenty dollars per song from the costumers, and we would normally cash out with only twenties. So when the Hungarians saw the smaller bills they asked me if I'd been charging less than twenty dollars per song. I said no. They then asked me where the smaller bills came from. I told them that I had bought myself a grilled cheese sandwich for lunch. They looked at me as if I had just casually confessed to committing an atrocity. The chauffer replied "Listen to me very carefully, you owe us thousands of dollars and until you pay that off, none of the money that you make is yours. Technically, you have spent my money, and I am not happy about that. Tomorrow you will make an extra fifty dollars as a penalty."

As determined as I was, my ever increasing debt to my 'employers' was demoralizing. I didn't understand how I was going to get ahead of these costs and the interest accruing on them.

Day and night we went to a coffee or sandwich place before and after our shifts where we were each given a sandwich and a can of pop. We worked 6 days a week from 11am to 6 am. I was 125lbs when I came to Canada. Two weeks after my arrival I weighed less than 90 lbs. I was extremely weak, sleep deprived and profoundly fatigued. We got a day off every Sunday only because you didn't make enough money to warrant going to the club on Sunday and instead we all spent the day shopping together. At night the girls would be given a plethora of drugs and new men would come over to drink in the motel and be entertained.

One Sunday I asked if I could stay in my room during one of the impromptu "parties" and I learned the next day that the Hungarians had given an 18-year-old girl five lines of pure cocaine. Before then she had never done a drug in her life, and neither had I.

I bumped into her seven years later. She was still in Canada, still addicted to drugs and still trying to get out of that life style. We talked about the "old days" and she was still terrified of even discussing how we escaped. When I brought up the possibility of her coming to testify for me, she started shaking and swearing and she said that there was no way she could - which crushed me. She was the only person who could corroborate my story who was still alive and in Canada.

At this point, Alfonzo was using me whenever he pleased and I was working twenty-one hour shifts, six days a week. I was mentally, physically and spiritually exhausted.
A few weeks had passed, and I heard the girls talking about going to other clubs and a few had actually told the Hungarians to take them, because there was no money in our current club which catered to low-income perverts.

In my current headspace, even the whisperings of a change - any change - lifted my spirits. I might be able to make money faster. I could put some distance between myself and my unsavory fumblings with Alphonso. I might actually be able to rest and regroup.

Chapter 4

At the end of the following week, we packed up and were off to the north end of Toronto to work in a place that was known for being packed with high paying customers. It was funded by biker money and was overseen by bikers. It definitely wasn't your average strip joint.

As we were moved to the new place, I got my first glimpse of Toronto beyond the stretch separating our motel from the first strip club I'd worked in.

Like a prisoner enjoying her first minute of designated yard time, I felt the fresh air and a sense of life and possibility returning to me. I wasn't sure where we were going, but I have a good memory and I tried to carefully watch the road and remember streets, buildings and landmarks. This became increasingly difficult the further we drove. Businesses and generic subdivisions began to repeat themselves, throwing off the landmark-based map I was trying to commit to my memory. The drive was also long enough for the chauffeurs to find time to entertain us with horror stories about Sasha and his colleagues beating up girls in Hungary, Germany, and the Ukraine.

Try as I might, I could never shield myself from the impact of these stories, and it was easy to see how it affected the other girls. Some became very emotional, and would talk back to the Hungarian chauffeurs. It wasn't very smart because I could see that they started to pay very close attention to the 'problem children' of the group.

When they opened their mouths, the chauffeurs listened. When they moved, they watched them closely. If their tone was undesirable, they would have their tones re-tuned.
And as this particular drive came to a halt, the violent stories halted with it. "There is a man inside who is watching you all." They said. "He is working for us. There are other Hungarian girls in this club, but you are not allowed to talk to them. If you do, our man will tell me immediately and you will be removed."

They told us to go inside, but they stayed in the car themselves. This was peculiar, as they had never left our sides until that moment. I filed this information away as interesting for the time being, not knowing how this shift in behavior was to impact my future plans. They said they'd be back at 6 a.m. to pick us up when the club closed. Three of us got dropped off but one girl remained with them. It was Alexandra, the one who taught me how to perform on my first day. She was working somewhere else and it seemed that the chauffeurs favored her over the rest of us, which was fine with me.

As we walked downstairs, three security guards immediately stopped us. These weren't bouncers and looked more like secret service. They said something to one of us who spoke some English and all three relayed her broken words through microphones strapped an inch in front of their lips.

A man in a suit promptly arrived and led us down a short carpeted hallway. I was mentally preparing myself for another "interview" but this man remained very professional and very direct. He asked for our work permits and told us the house rules:

"You must go on stage every hour for three songs. By the second song you must be naked. Keep your purse with you at all times. No drugs in the club at any time. Stay away from the other girls. If you need help call the guards. There are 3 VIP rooms and they all have a different price. The drink prices are different in each room and money is made primarily on drinks, so make sure your customers are drinking. Your locker will be cleaned every week so no shoes or old dresses in them."

As he gave us a tour it was hard to miss the grandeur of the place. It had multiple levels and seemed very busy compared to my first club. This place was all marble countertops and crushed velvet pillows under smoky blue lighting. The women working looked strong, like they went to the gym in hopes of perfecting their craft of strip-tease and burlesque.

This club was for the big players and it was staffed with experienced girls. We were told by the manager to stay away from them for our own sake. Knives, mace and pepper spray were typically found in a seasoned prostitute's purse.

Our tour continued to the three VIP rooms and the room where we would pick up our towels. (You had to have a little white towel to put on the customers lap, and it would glow in the black light so that the bouncers could see it.) Of course it was the law, but the reality was that it was routinely ignored. There were hardly any girls who would not let the customers touch them. If you didn't let them touch you, they'd simply get another girl who would.

Up in the DJ booth, we met the DJ. He seemed completely foreign to the environment he worked in. He was a total character in an almost novelty sized cowboy hat and ponytail. The sight of him almost made me laugh - an honest laugh – which was an impulse I hadn't had in weeks.

He asked the other girls for their stage names and when he came to me, I looked at him and said the only American name that came to my head, Alysson, my favorite character from Melrose Place. He looked me in the eye and smiled at my answer. "Alysson it is." He said that he would call our name one song before it was our turn to go on and we should look over the CD collection to pick three songs we liked. The first has to be fast, the second has to be somewhat slower, and the last has to be a slinking, suspenseful slow number.

The club was full of customers and the main stage had a big runway with 3 different wings, each equipped with its own pole. Men came in for bachelor parties, and women were a regular part of the clientele here.

For the first time in weeks I felt the fear, which had become a constant companion, subside a degree or two. The grandeur of the club and the forced anonymity between the girls allowed me to focus on me, without the threat of an owner pulling me into his office at random to satisfy his whims. I could tolerate my chauffeurs for smaller designated portions of the day, and I was beginning to feel more relaxed with the idea of being naked in front of strangers. However, when my song began to play and "Cowboy J" the DJ began bellowing my name like a boxing announcer, my legs would always weaken and threaten to collapse.

Chapter 5

Weeks passed quickly and I was finally making the kind of money I wanted to, but physically, earning $1000 a day in a strip club is draining, especially when you're only drinking non-alcoholic blue lagoons and cans of pop. My eighty-nine pound figure could only handle so much physical effort, junk food and sleep deprivation. As a result, I lost more weight than was considered healthy. How could I have been stripping in Canada for almost two months, at some points making $1000 a day and still be in debt, I wondered.

One night at the motel, the six girls, the chauffeurs and I got together in my room for a "family meeting." A tired looking girl named Ersebet looked spooked. She had the eyes of someone at the end of a long journey, like she had just come in the door from across the world. "You know this isn't right." She spoke quickly. "Why haven't I paid off my debt yet? There isn't much time left for me if I keep up like this. You know a man slapped me in the club today and he said he would come back tomorrow for me and I better play nice. The coffee maker never works in my room and I never have any money or time or privacy for myself." She became more and more frantic. "I'm going to find a calculator or an accountant or a road straight to the cop shop if this mess doesn't get sorted."

My first reaction was to want to silence her verbally, but she continued, "And I'm sure the cops wouldn't be happy to see how many girls you buy and sell everyday either. This really isn't the most lawful operation I've seen." My second reaction was a desire to silence her physically, but it was too late and the words had already come out. The bolder chauffeur took her passport and ripped out some pages that included her work permit. They both rose above her whimpering form and screamed and berated her while we watched, seated calmly on the bedsides.

The next morning on our way to the club we overheard more stories about Sasha than usual. The implied threat was ever present, and repeated all the more often and with more detail whenever any of us broke rank and questioned the status quo.

Apparently, a girl's family member was set on fire in a small village after the girl merely mentioned the police. They pondered loudly about what should happen with Ersebet, seeing as she wouldn't be able to work without a permit or travel without a passport now. I realized that we weren't taking the same roads as we usually did towards the Club as we slowly pulled into an industrial area, inching around hidden corners, far from the clientele that we would normally entertain.

We finally stopped at a dilapidated building that looked like it belonged in an old western ghost town. Lurching around to face us in the back seat, the chauffeurs instructed that I and another girl follow them inside.

The girl accompanying me knew the drill and immediately went to work, striding into the back office of the place where a familiar man sat on a large chair. The chauffeurs left us alone and as the other girl brushed back past me, I asked her what our prerogative was here. "This place is owned by Alfonzo and he needed some girls on Mondays."

"Well, what am I suppose to do here, office work?" I asked. She laughed and walked me out of the front office and into each room that lined the sterile corridor.

They were nice rooms with candles, showers and massage tables. Clothed work! But as the tour continued to the supply room where the towels and other work products were kept, including condoms, I almost fainted.

As she showed me the laundry room it spun before my eyes and I had to sit down by the door. She thrust a price list under my nose. A bikini massage was 60 dollars for half an hour and a full body (nude) massage was 80 dollars for half an hour. "And you're aware that bikini is a blow job and full body is sex." She said, matter of factly. Recoiling and looking her in the eyes, I said, "I am not a prostitute." "Yeah, that's nice. Tell that to the boss. So, the next client is yours" she retorted.

"Listen, can I just do laundry and you take the clients today?" I earnestly asked.

She laughed and turned away, "Ok, honey, just do the laundry."

For the entire morning I did everything I could to avoid the clients while she took care of them all, but I knew that this wouldn't last. Finally, my lack of an agency, the previous evening's events and my morning dose of Sasha stories eventually had their desired effect.

Three young Russian speaking guys walked into the building. The other girl looked at me and said, "Take them. Make your money - it'll be quick, in and out!" After pouring over the price list as if they were ordering their next meal, all three pointed to full body massage. Reluctantly, I showed them into the room I had been assigned. I motioned for one to follow me, but since I didn't speak English at the time, as I proceeded to get 'ready,' all three walked into the room at the same time, which wasn't expected. I didn't have the language skills to protest and say that I could only handle one a time, so I panicked and didn't refuse.

I thought I might be able to get away with just massaging each of them for twenty minutes so that time would run out before anything else could happen. Keeping a close eye on the clock the entire time, the minutes passed excruciatingly slow. I could sense their growing impatience, so I wasn't altogether surprised when one of them motioned for me to get on top of the massage table. I was 'helped' up on the table and immediately stripped of my clothing. Naked and lying on my back as they stood around me, I felt like a piece of meat. I wanted to die.

Each one of the young men removed their shirts, and the first one removed his pants. He ripped off my panties and without any warning entered me violently. Being a smaller girl with limited sexual experience, it was painful. I pushed against his will to enter me, but it wasn't an option. Freezing, I was lying on the table with my legs wide open and soul bared to all.

While one pleasured himself inside me, the other two kept busy violating other parts of my body, forcing me to please them with my hands and mouth. To cope with the reality of the situation, I closed my eyes and ordered my muscles to relax. In the meantime, the clients changed positions, taking turns pleasuring themselves. Mercifully, the girl was right. It was quick. These men were 'finished' with me in less than thirty minutes.

Every part of my body was sore, especially my groin. I immediately rinsed off the shame by getting in the shower as quickly as I could. I glanced over at myself, but didn't recognize the girl I saw in the mirror. Timea, the girl who sang in front of an audience of 1,500 during school celebrations, and who volunteered at the library every evening just so that she wouldn't have to go home to hear her parents screaming at one another, seemed like a distant memory. I realized that my difficult childhood, familial dysfunction and alcoholic father didn't seem so intolerable all of the sudden. A strong knock on the door brought me back - it was the hostess of the parlor telling me to hurry up.

"You took all three? You don't have to let them do what ever they want, honey. Next time charge them extra if they want extra favors." Favors seemed like a peculiar term for the exchange, when pain was preventing me from stepping into my underwear. A third girl showed me where the lubrication was kept.

After three more hours of painful laundry and self deception, I had to "do" another client for twelve minutes and he left. When I try to recall him now, I can't even remember what he looked like. The chauffeurs came and picked me up around six and as soon as they got there, I surprised them. I immediately spoke up telling them that I'd never go back. Wasn't I usually the good girl who never put a word in edgewise?

Over the past few weeks however, I'd been taking mental notes and quickly understood that these were not smart men, they were only intimidating because they preyed on people's immediate fears. They had trigger words, much like we did. They'd say words like family, death, problem children and we'd listen; while we'd say words like police, escape, testify and they'd listen. Not wanting them to listen to me, I learned what not to say. But I needed survivable conditions to exist in, so I told them that I would make much less there then I could in the club. It was their language. They responded well and decided to keep me working the rest of the night back in my strange sanctuary of the ritzy club.

The woman who worked the coat check saw my state as I entered the club and immediately gave me her lipstick and some moisturizer for my face. She was African-Canadian with peaceful hazel eyes and often taught me English words that I needed to know in order to competently work in the club. She would give me medicine when I had headaches or stomach pain. She always seemed like the silver lining on my cloudy days.

Becoming accustomed to twenty hour days, six days a week was nearly impossible and the coat check girl could tell. She would let me sleep in the VIP room so that I had an extra half hour or so of sleep before my shift and, to my delight, no one harassed me about it or even brought it up, not the chauffeurs, not the bouncers, not the owner. They just let me do my own thing. I didn't tell them for a week and soon realized that they were lying about people always watching the girls. They had no clue about what I was doing all day, so why couldn't I just leave?

The next day after my first dance, I decided to take a chance. I picked up my clothes and glided into the change room, breathing feverishly as I changed into my street clothes and walked out the backdoor. No one followed me. I walked to the main street and made sure that the chauffeurs weren't in the parking lot.

I walked a block. A car horn honked loudly and my heart sunk with the sound of it. A woman crossed the street yelling my stage name, but turned out to be attracting the attention of an Alice who had matched my stride and was passing me on the sidewalk. Seconds felt like hours of dreamtime and I got weaker with each step. Air became colder and I felt increasingly more vulnerable, lost in this unfamiliar territory.

The brainwashing had clearly worked and I began making my way back to the club after only ten minutes in public. I knew that I would be safer in the club than anywhere else and I resigned myself to return to the hand that fed, or rather, barely sustained me.

As I slid subtly back into the club, a grey haired woman in a black dress stormed past me with her daughter. They mumbled to each other in Hungarian but I didn't say anything, I didn't know who they were or what they were doing here.

They were in the office while I changed but burst into the change room, frightening the hell out of my already tested nerves.

With a bouncer, they found and cut the lock off a locker. Over the sound of the locker banging, I heard the older woman begin to grieve. I watched them put everything that was in the locker into a black garbage bag and quickly make their exit.

I learned later that the Hungarian woman was a mother of a dancer I had seen at the club and eaten with numerous times. She hadn't been in contact with home for some time and when her mother inquired with the local police, they identified her as an overdose case whose body had been retrieved from the subway the night before. During the next few days, I constantly surveyed myself; questioning what I was doing and how well I really knew anyone. How could she have overdosed? Did she even do hard drugs?

It was almost two and a half months that I'd been a dancer and occasional prostitute, a far stretch from the job and life I once had in Budapest. I sacrificed my own television show to come here, left a loving boyfriend, and for what? I was falling further and further from myself, but the end was in sight.

I quietly pondered the spaces between the stars on a quiet ride back to the motel one morning. "What's wrong?" asked the chauffeur. "You know my flight home is three weeks away." I replied, ignoring his patronizing attempts at compassion. "You're finally making money and we're about to get an apartment with three rooms, so never mind that," he said. "We can finally have a little consistency, eh? A real working girl's routine, how's that sound? A little nest of your own, too! How's that sound?" he asked hopefully.

I chose my words well, "I love the money, that's for sure. But I miss my Mama, you understand. I think it is time for me to go back home."

"You could never make this kind of money at home," he countered casually. "And me and the girls would all miss you too much. Plus we've got the apartment. Then there's the new car on the way for driving a princess like you around; that has to be paid for before you can start chipping away at your debt for the plane tickets. It's simple accounting really, so don't get too anxious about that flight home just yet."

Since I'd started, I'd been documenting my daily figures and calculated that I had made about $18,000 in the last two months. He had understood that I may have paid about $2,000 to them and still had at least $3,000 left in debts.

Without warning I saw him dead behind my eyes. Clearly for the first time in a long time, I was ready to be the killer of every last one of these tireless thieves. Never have I felt so much anger. Never have I visualized the killing of another human being but there was no way out for me. I was cornered. I could not confront him now, but armed with this knowledge, I felt released from my debts. "I do really think I'm getting the hang of my stage show, learning how to play the crowd, you know. It's fun." I said softly.

That night, the chauffeur asked me to collect money from the other girls. It was an unwarranted sign of trust, so I agreed. The small Hungarian, Ersebet, who had been staying in my room for the few weeks I'd slept at the club, was nowhere to be found. After a half hour of pacing in my room and deliberating about what to say, I returned to the chauffeur's quarters and asked if they had picked her up from the club. He shook his head no, got on his phone and brusquely shooed me out.

The drive the following morning felt surreal, without the always talkative Ersebet with us, conversation was awkward and stilted. None of us knew where she was and frankly we were scared to ask. That same day as we made our way home from the club under a pumpkin sunrise, the chauffeurs told us that our little girlfriend had finally fucked with the wrong people.

When we asked what happened, they said, "Don't worry she isn't breathing anymore."

We looked at each other with masked disbelief and in this moment of stifled laughter and near patronization, I began to believe that she had in fact escaped. If she did, did Sasha even exist? Do they really know my family and would they try and find them if I did do something brave? How loose was this leash around my neck?

I gripped my purse tightly as we accelerated down the road and thought about the plane ticket waiting for me, safely in the night stand of my motel room. My flight was leaving in two weeks on August 18th. For the next week it was an all consuming idea. In dreams, I would flee and then get caught, run and then trip. I was sleeping fitfully, vacillating wildly between hope and fear, and barely functioning when I was awake. But I began to plan my departure.

In the club I had to stay busy so I always had my dictionary on hand. The DJ was always eager to help me communicate and after a few days of playful language exchange with him, I spilled a very broken but truthful version of who I was and why I was working at the club. From the coercion and moral bankruptcy of my captors to the basics about my loved ones back home, he heard it all and to my relief was sympathetic.

I told the DJ and a sympathetic night shift bouncer about my plan to escape the week before my flight and that I would need some help that I could trust. They both knew I was a gamble, but my sincerity won them over and they offered to help in any way that they could.

Walking into the club the next day with a duffel bag full of everything I owned wouldn't exactly be a smooth exit, so I had to take my time and worked quietly in order to avoid suspicion.

Day-by-day, I smuggled my things from the motel to my locker. Bits of clothes, a Lion King stuffed animal I got from my boyfriend when I left Hungary, a pair of shoes, a few plastic cases of makeup and the rest of my personal belongings. Four days later, I was ready to move.

After a familiar breakfast of pop and a stale sandwich, I had images circling in my head about all the horrific things that could happen if my plan didn't succeed. I saw my lifeless body in a garbage can and my mom in a mortuary identifying my body sprinkled with cigarette burns. I was anchored by the thought that if I beat the chauffeurs back to Hungary before their arrival on the 20th, I could go straight to the Hungarian police and have them caught at the airport.

In the front seat, the chauffeurs talked excitedly about the new group of girls who were being recruited in Hungary. These faceless and voiceless girls, and the thought that I could help them, would be my motivation for years to come.

When we got to the club, I told them that some big hockey group was coming tonight and I'd be occupied until at least 6 a.m., if not longer. My body was shaking. I told them to take their time coming back and smiled forcefully. Since I decided to escape four days ago, I had yet to sleep.

I weakly got out of the car and sauntered in the front door and then headed straight for the DJ booth where he held out his house keys for me. The DJ then signaled for the bouncer. The bouncer knew what he had to do but didn't show it. He walked with his head down until he got to the pay phone by the window and while watching the chauffeurs pull out of the lot, he called a black limo taxi for me.

By the time I had my stuff out of my locker and was down the hallway and out the back door, the cab was waiting. I almost fainted when the DJ burst open the back door to talk to the driver. He gave him a stack of cash and fast directions. Nodding to me, he closed the car door and re-entered the club.

Sitting in the backseat I remember thinking to myself: "If he only knew what I was a part of right now and just how much his cab and this ride meant to me. If he only knew this was the first time I've felt free since I stepped off a plane at Pearson three month's ago; the first time I didn't have to take my clothes off at command, or the first car ride in Canada I had experienced without the accompaniment of psychologically debilitating stories about girls being killed and tortured. If the cab driver only knew how happy I was to be overhearing a conversation in a language other than Hungarian or English."

I fell asleep to the sound of the driver chatting away in a language which I still can't identify all these years later. It was sunset when we left the city and dark by the time we arrived at our destination. All I knew for certain is that I was headed north. We stopped in front of a large brick house and I remember my hands shaking so badly it took me a good five minutes to open the front door. While I was trying to get into the house, I had this nagging feeling that someone was following or watching me so I was relieved when I finally made my way inside. I found myself in a dark bedroom sitting on a water bed for the first time in my life, which was a novelty, but at this point, a sleeping bag on the floor would've sufficed.

I called the club and talked with Jimmy letting him know I had arrived safely and to thank him. I couldn't understand what he was saying in response, so the conversation was brief. I headed back to the bedroom, and before closing my eyes noticed that it was 10:30 p.m. on Wednesday night. I couldn't have been more than a matter of seconds before I was fast asleep. For the first time in months I was warm and safe. The next thing I remembered was waking up and looking at the clock. It was 1:00 pm on Thursday. The windows were covered with huge, dark blue curtains making the room as dark in the daytime as it was at night. I had slept for fifteen hours straight.

I awoke to a beautiful sight. Peering up at me from the bedside were two gorgeous Huskies. I had never seen such beautiful animals in all my life. They stood motionless like two guardian angels with their light blue eyes glowing in the dark. I wanted to reach out to pet them, but I was too exhausted to move. I noticed a tray next to the bed holding a glass of water, a sandwich and a note. It said, "I was here. Sleep as much as you like. Call me when you need to. The phone number is…."

I was so parched and exhausted that even the thought of lifting the glass of water to my lips was a struggle. The last thing I remember before drifting off to sleep again was the sight of those two pairs of eyes looking up at me as I fell into another deep sleep. Three a.m. I had slept another fourteen hours straight. I didn't know what day it was anymore, but I remember feeling a very warm and fuzzy sensation near my feet. My two guardian angels, the Huskies, were sleeping soundly on the bed providing me with a much needed and previously unavailable sense of protection and unconditional love.

With my animal escort leading the way, I returned from the restroom and promptly fell back into bed. I thought that maybe I'd eat the sandwich, but again, just the thought of doing anything, be it ever so basic, exhausted me. I put my head on the pillow and was out again in a matter of minutes. Six p.m. I had slept another twelve hours. My energy was slowly returning so I got out of the bed, alert for the first time in days, and I opened the curtains and was welcomed by the sight of a huge green lawn. I called for my husky guardians, but they weren't around.

Standing in the shower a short while later, the realization that I'd be home in less than a week's time dawned on me. I thought about my cat and my family, but for some reason I couldn't imagine looking either my pet or my loved ones in the eyes. Surprised I wasn't more excited, I knew something fundamental had changed. I had become a different person. I opened my sports bag as I was getting ready to leave when I saw my Lion King doll. A deep sadness welled up inside of me. The sweet gesture of giving me a stuffed animal suddenly seemed very childlike and inappropriate. I wasn't up for crying, so I shoved the stuffed animal to the bottom of my bag, stifling related thoughts about my new identity, and I proceeded to get ready to leave.

Driving back to the city after being picked up by the club's driver, Canada's natural beauty became apparent to me for the first time. As we drove, I took in every passing image. The limo pulled up at the back of Pink Dolls and dropped me off. As soon as I walked inside, a bouncer pulled me aside. Looking worried, he tried to tell me something, but I didn't understand him. As I was making my way back to the dressing room, I froze dead in my tracks. One of the girls from my group was sitting on top of a table waiting for me. I thought to myself, "Oh my God - they're here to get me!" Melinda confirmed that Josef and Sandor had sent her inside to look for me.

"If you'll follow me outside, they'll forget everything and no one will get hurt," she said.

"I'm afraid I can't do that", I replied without hesitation - my foray into freedom had given me the conviction to withstand their coercion.

"Then you know they're going to get really angry and you'll be in a world of trouble. I'm not going to tell them that I saw you in here, but just be careful because they will come back. They know this is the only place you could be and they'll come back" she said.

She slipped me a phone number and told me that it was Andrea's, a Hungarian bartender who worked at a different strip club, and that I should call her if I needed a place to stay. I could sleep on her couch until I left Canada. I gave her a big hug and thanked her for not giving me up. I thought it was the last time I'd see her. I sat in the dressing room too terrified to leave. Since I didn't have any money or a plan for the next five days, I forced myself to put on my dancing clothes to earn cash for a motel, cab fare and pocket money for the journey home. I danced all night. I wasn't proud of myself, as a matter of fact I felt ashamed while doing it, but I had to survive and reassured myself with the knowledge that I wouldn't have to do this again.

I pulled out the piece of paper with Andrea's phone number and called. She gave me her address which was about an hour away from the club. When I arrived at her house, I was surprised to see another girl staying with her. She was my second roommate, the one who smoked a lot of marijuana and got roughed up for speaking her mind. This was the same girl we were told wasn't 'breathing' anymore. For the past two months, I had thought she was dead, but when I saw her, she was very much alive. She had been working in another strip club across town, and was heading home herself later that month. She was sympathetic to what I had gone through and agreed it was awful, and hoped I was getting out too. She assured me we were safe staying at Andrea's even though she'd sometimes score cocaine for Josef and Sandor. We both felt confident that she wouldn't blow our cover.

After settling in the living room and talking for a couple of hours, we both decided to crash. She then went to her club for work and I went back to mine. We agreed to meet back here in the morning to chat again. We both woke up fairly late the next day but agreed to head out for a 'normal' lunch. Naomi knew the area and spoke more English than I did, so I felt comfortable. While we were deciding what to eat, the phone rang. I thought it was Andrea so I answered. A very familiar male's voice asked for Andrea. I said she wasn't home, but would be back later. As I spoke, I suddenly realized it was Josef. Panicked, I signaled with my hands and feet to get Naomi's attention. "Josef is on the phone!" I whispered.

She motioned for me to hang up. As I was hanging up I heard Josef saying "Timea! Timea! Is that you? I'm coming to get you!" I slammed the phone down and starting screaming, "They know I'm here. They're coming to get me."

She immediately said, "Get dressed. Let's get out of here, now!"

I threw on some clothes, grabbed my bag and was just about ready to run out the door when someone pressed the downstairs buzzer. Naomi ran to the TV monitor and saw it was Josef and Sandor standing in the lobby. They apparently knew where Andrea lived and were only five minutes away when they had called. As we watched the monitor in sheer panic, we saw that someone had let them into the building. I looked at Naomi and said "We can't go outside now. And they won't be able to get into the apartment, so as long as we stay in here, we'll be ok, right?"

As we triple-checked the locks, we stood silent in our tracks until we heard a loud bang on the door. "Timea, we know you're in there you piece of shit. We're very disappointed. Be warned. We're going to break the door down and break your bones. You shit head! You think you can play us? Your mother will be very disappointed when she finds out that you're a whore."

Naomi panicked and locked herself in the bathroom. I went out onto the eight floor balcony to see if there was an escape route. I noticed I could climb across to the next balcony and the next balcony, and so forth. Without thinking, I kicked off my shoes and climbed over the adjoining balcony. Not stopping there, I climbed through yet another balcony forcing myself not to look down.

Adrenalin and fight or flight instinct kicked in leaving me no time to consider the potential danger. I climbed across three balcony rails and luckily none of the owners were home at the time. Crouching in the corner of a stranger's balcony, I closed my eyes and started to pray. I prayed to God begging that Josef and Sandor wouldn't find me. I clasped my hands so tightly I thought I'd break my own fingers. The fear was more intense than anything I'd ever felt before in my life.

About twenty minutes later, I heard them talking downstairs in the parking lot. Through a thin slit in the balcony railing, I saw them get into their car and take off. I knew I had to make my way back, so I gathered my courage. Without the benefit of an adrenalin rush, climbing across those balcony rails was terrifying. I finally made it back to Andrea's balcony in one piece. Naomi was nowhere to be found.

Chapter 6

Making sure the coast was clear; I caught a cab back to Pink Dolls. I tried to explain to Mark and Jimmy what had happened, asking them to keep an eye on the front door to ensure that Josef and Sandor would not return. I needed the money, so I changed into my dancing clothes and tried to keep my mind busy. One of the bouncers pointed me towards a girl who I had often seen in the club, but whom I had never spoken to. I was surprised to find out that she was Hungarian too. Her English was so perfect I thought she was Canadian. She asked me why the bouncer thought we should talk - and as I had trusted the bouncer, I trusted her, too. We sat down in a quiet corner of the club and I told her my story.

Christine didn't look like she belonged in the club environment. She was pretty. Her hair and makeup always looked so high-end, as if she had stepped out of the pages of ELLE magazine. She mixed Hungarian with English, and assumed I understood her. After I told her my story, she said I should have come to her much earlier as she had rescued many girls over the past several years. Calmly and confidently, she shed light on my terrible circumstances. She knew the drill and how these individuals worked. She mentioned most of the threats were just brainwashing, and that Josef and his group had no real power over me. "But what about the guy they call Sasha? You should hear what they tell us about him. He sounds like an evil man," I said.

"Don't believe a word of it, Timea. It's all a bunch of lies. They're just trying to scare you into doing what they want and to keep you quiet" I thought to myself, 'well…..it worked.'

We spoke for about two hours and I was reassured by her confidence. Just being in Christine's strong presence made me feel safe. Knowing I didn't have a place to stay for the next several days, she graciously offered her place to me and I took her up on it. At the end of our shift at 6:00 am, two bouncers escorted us to her car and we took off. Her house was a 45-minute drive from the club. There was a spare room in the basement with a bed and desk. It was perfect. She brought me clean sheets and wished me a good night's sleep. Christine's kind sanctuary was another port in the storm.

I woke up to the smell of fresh coffee. I made my way upstairs to find Christine making breakfast. I was surprised when I noticed the size of her milk carton. It was just like the movies. Even the shape of the bread reminded me of my favorite movie, Kramer vs. Kramer. I'd seen that movie dozens of times and flashed on the breakfast scene where Dustin Hoffman's character is attempting to make French toast for his son for the first time. The sight of milk jugs and bread was reassuring. Seemingly unimportant things in everyday life now seemed so special, reassuring in their familiar domesticity.

We ended up talking for about five hours that day. She told me all about the club, the bouncers, and management. She filled me in on a lot of behind the scenes details I wasn't aware of. It was the first time I actually got to know the place in all its Technicolor glory. "What does it mean when some of the clients say they want to go upstairs with me?" I asked.

"There are private rooms on the second floor where some of the girls have sex for money and charge anywhere from $300 to $400 per client," she informed me. I was shocked, but I was finally able to put that piece of the puzzle in its place. I had been repeatedly asked over the past two and a half months by customers if I would go upstairs with them, but I didn't know what it meant, and had always said no.

Chapter 7

My nerves were shredded as we traveled from rural Ontario to the more populated outskirts of Toronto near Pearson airport. I was sweating while checking my bags, perspiring when I went through security and almost dehydrated by the time we left the tarmac. The only thing I kept with me on the flight from my checked baggage was the Lion King stuffed animal which kept me company for the duration of the flight.

During the ten hour flight home, I was coming down with a very bad flu. My body was on fire, I could barely keep my eyes open, I was shivering, could hardly talk and I was sweating like crazy. Twelve years later, I still remember that flu – it was one of the worst I had ever had. As my nerves and health were getting the better of me, I decided that I should simply go home to bed and rest before going to the Hungarian police to intercept my chauffeurs. I would have a two day window before they arrived so I could still talk to the police once I had rested and catch them at the airport.

By the time we arrived in Budapest and I found my luggage, I was weaker then ever. I was classically malnourished and weakening fast. On the edge of fainting I could hardly see where I was going as I inched forward in line and made my way to the Hungarian customs officer. All I could think of was my bed and my cat. I handed over my passport to the officer, who scanned the details over and over again. I knew he was getting suspicious so I stopped him.

"Yes, it's a fake passport," I said.

"Excuse me?" He was analyzing the numbers and my photo deeply, so I helped him, detailing exactly how it was made. He said, "Are you feeling alright Ms. Benedek?"

"That's not me. My name is Timea E. Nagy and I'd like to speak to your supervisor. I'm a human trafficking victim and the men who gave me this passport are arriving in this airport in two days with documentation describing all the money that I've paid to them over the past three months in a foreign strip club."

He led me to another room and sat me down. Given that it was the Hungarian long weekend, I didn't think anyone would be available to hear my story. After a short wait however, eight officers with guns and dogs stopped right in front of me and asked me to rise and follow them. I remember wondering if all of this was necessary for dealing with a twenty year old who had travelled with a fake passport. We walked down to the basement of the airport and into a holding cell that they no longer used. There was a long table where the officers had taken a seat and no one said a word to me. I sat down. I rallied under the strength of my conviction. I knew that I was clearly a victim here, so I was eager to tell my story to the authorities, no matter how tired or sick I was.

They all pulled out notepads and asked me to explain the conditions of how I attained my fake passport. From beginning to end, up and down, I told them what happened.

"Interesting," a quiet officer said. "Yes very interesting," said another. "Why should we believe a word of this?"

"Because it's the truth." I said frantically.

"But whose truth is it? Is it Teresa Benedek's' truth or, what is it, Timea Nagy's truth?"

"It's mine, Timea Nagy's." A choke dashed up my throat.

"Ok, I find that hard to believe to be honest," said the female officer of the group. "Why would you stay in Canada for so long after you saw the conditions of work? You're a smart girl who, apparently, had her own television show in Budapest. Everything was going well for you here and you just decided to drop it all and strip and hook at illegal sex parlors in a foreign country? I think you were joyriding."

They told me that for now, they were going to take my statement and detain me in a holding cell until the Hungarians arrived and I could somehow prove my story. Otherwise, I'd be going to a formal trial and on to jail in a Hungarian prison.

All I could think about were my cats during the transfer to what would be my cell for the night. I had my Lion King doll tucked into my chest as we wandered down the block to my new quarters. If Canada was bad, this was worse. I was getting sicker by the minute and the cell was freezing, small, and filled with black mold. The entire time I was in the cell, I don't think I blinked until hours later when a detective from the initial meeting showed up and asked that I come with him.

He made some small talk as we shuttled to another section of the airport, but I remained silent in sleep deprived astonishment. We crossed the parking lot under a terribly bright sun. To say I was jetlagged would be an understatement. At this point, I was still just a criminal in their eyes, and he was treating me like one. I took notice of how dated Hungarian architecture was compared to the Canadian facilities I'd just left as I sat in the office watching the detective ease into his chair, prepare a typewriter and begin asking questions.

Immediately, I could tell that he didn't believe me and frankly it seemed like he didn't care what answers I gave. That was until the part where I was told him that I had to dance naked for my money. He perked up and stopped typing, alert for the first time in our interview. "How was that?" he asked coyly.

"Embarrassing," I retorted quickly.
"You do have all the required features for a stripper: beautiful face, nice breasts…" He stood up. "You're not wearing a bra right now are you?"

"What?" I asked, thinking that I must have misunderstood.

"Your tits," he said. "They sit so naturally under your shirt, you wouldn't need a bra anyways." He began walking towards my chair.

"Is that part of the statement, officer?" I asked, looking up at him.

"I don't know, Is it?" he replied smugly. "How about you show me some of those moves of yours."

He got up from his desk and stood directly in front of me. I thought that he was going to touch me, but instead he asked me to stand up and show him some exotic dance moves. Sick, freezing and sweating, I couldn't believe this was happening. I don't remember exactly how, but I ended up standing up and facing the wall. What happened next was unthinkable. He undressed me. When a colleague walked in, I thought it would stop, but I was wrong. I felt someone grab my breasts from behind. Since I was facing the wall, I couldn't see who it was. Hands were groping me when all of the sudden I felt something enter me and it wasn't a body part. It was cold and long. I turned my head, but Officer Elek and his partner told me not to. I felt faint as I was violated by a large cold object which was forced into me several times. I knew I was being damaged because I felt an extremely sharp pain running all the way up my spine. I screamed from the pain only to hear him say, "It's a long weekend and no one is around."

It has been ten years since this happened and I still haven't forgiven Hungary and her authorities for enabling this act of violence and their horrific abuse of my trust. I would rather die than relive this and I will never return to my homeland because of it. I was bleeding and I couldn't think.

As I write this, I have no memory of what happened after that event. All I remember is the pain that has stayed with me ever since that day. Sometimes it comes when I'm lifting heavy bags at the grocery store or during my period, and sometimes it comes when I butter morning toast or steep my tea. It doesn't matter. This pain has remained with me ever since and, of course, each episode of pain brings forth associations from my memory that I would rather not relive.

Chapter 8

Finally, I received news that the Hungarians had arrived at the airport and been taken into custody. Like I told them they would, the police found documents containing my stage name and details about the money I and the other girls had been paying our captors.

This verified my story as far as the fake passport was concerned, so the detectives drove me home. I didn't let anyone know I was arriving and I hoped that my brother wouldn't be around to see me getting dropped off by two cops. I got out of the car and heard them say that they'd be back in two days with some more information about my court case because I was to testify against my Hungarian chauffeurs. If I didn't, I'd be charged and put in jail for the use of my fake passport.

I was bombarded with familiar images from what seemed like another life as I struggled to lift my luggage out of the trunk and drag it to the elevator, slumping against the cold wall and pushing the button for my floor. Fumbling for my house keys, I found them and gave them a long look. These keys had reminded me of who I was and where I came from in my darkest hours overseas. Opening the door, I inhaled deeply, flooding the chasm of my lungs with the very smell I tried to recall so many nights in the motel room before sleeping the scant five hours I was allotted to rest and recuperate.

My cats ran towards me and I had never been happier to see them. I hugged them and called my brother's name. When he didn't answer I got ready for bed and fell asleep in seconds. I awoke to a sharp pang of pain which was the result of my experience with the Hungarian police and I went to the bathroom to investigate it. I saw the old makeup bag that I had used for my television show and I became very nostalgic. I had to poke around for other things in the house to verify that I was, in fact, actually home.

I prepared some tea using a huge mug from my collection. My brother used to say that when I drank from this oversized mug, my entire face would disappear in it. I smiled and missed him terribly. I saw my brother's laundry in a basket and took out a t-shirt, holding it tight and breathing deeply the familiar scents I missed so dearly. However I still didn't call my mom or brother to tell them that I had arrived. I didn't know what to say or how to say it. My voice sounded horrible and would only worry them, so I decided to wait a little bit longer.

After spending a lonely night in my old home next to my cats torturing myself with images and feelings from the past three months, I vowed not to talk about what happened to me in Canada unless I needed to by law. Everything would just go away if I forgot about it and focused on getting my old life back.

My brother came home and was very surprised to see me. He asked me why I hadn't called him from the airport for a ride home but I silenced him with a lame excuse about jetlag. "Did you make any money for the rent?" he asked. I replied without explanation, "No, I'm sorry. I didn't."

"So you just went to Canada for fun then didn't you?" he asked accusatorially.

"No, now wait." I interjected, too late.

"I think I understand just fine. You went on a vacation and had the time of your life while I didn't have enough money to put food in the fridge. You needed an escape from all of these bills, so you left. And then you just come back as if you'd never left."

I couldn't tell him what happened, so I lowered my head. "Why didn't you call more? Twice in three months, are you serious? The party must have been really good over there, Timea. Mom didn't stop worrying about you the whole time, you know." He also told me that everyone at the station where I had worked thought I had become a drug addled whore in Toronto. My boyfriend had to be hospitalized due to stress because I never updated him as to my whereabouts. How did all of this happen? I felt worse then ever.

It is one thing when the police don't believe you, but when your family and friends start to turn on you, it turns you against yourself. He continued to yell at me until I couldn't take it, and I told him to leave me alone.

With my heart heavy and what felt like the weight of the world on my shoulders, it became apparent that I had to get the whole ordeal off my chest or it would consume me. My boyfriend was the jealous type and had always complained that I flirted too much, but I didn't care. The secret of what had happened to me was too great to bear alone any longer and I made the cross town trip to see him.

When I first saw him, I was terrified. He was considerably taller then me and spoke like a rusty old militant. I tried to be brave and start slowly, incrementally telling him more and more detailed pieces of the nightmare that I'd survived. It was when I told him about my shift in the massage parlor that he silenced me with a turn of his heel and an accusatory finger pointed towards my face.

He moved back quickly in disgust, looked at me and explained that he didn't believe a word of it. He said that I was a liar who had lost her mind. He said that if I expected him to trust me, I was self-deluding. But I had had enough of people not believing what I had to say, enough of people yelling at me. I had enough of people abusing me in countless ways and I couldn't take any more of it.

I asked him to take me home and as he cursed me and wrung words like 'embarrassment' and 'burden' dry, I could only glare at the horizon that led to my house, trying in vain to shield myself from the pain that his words caused. I closed his car door behind me and I never saw him again. Walking inside, I wondered, "Could I disappear behind my bedroom door? If I had no more visitors or contact with anyone who knew me, would I cease to exist? What if I killed myself? How did three months in Canada turn my home life, work life and state of fruitful youth into a suicidal wasteland? Why was my skull pounding as if my mind wanted to escape?"

I didn't leave my house for two days and didn't have much contact with my brother. However I did mistake my heartbeat for his footsteps from time to time, sometimes not being able to tell the difference. The following morning the working week began, and it seemed as though all of Budapest was shuffling into work early, except me. I didn't have a job and we still owed a lot of money in back rent. The rumors and shame I'd meet at the station were compelling enough reasons to keep me away and I gradually sunk into an unemployed and depressive state.

After everything I had fought through to come home, I felt myself slowly submitting to the negative opinions about me held by the people nearest to me. My ex-boyfriend, my brother and my former work colleagues thought I was an irresponsible whore. During those dark days, I found myself agreeing with them.

Under the covers my eyes searched blankly around the room and my mind for an anchor, an affirmation, a call to action. Then, I was startled by a knock on the apartment's front door. Timidly, I looked through the peephole, preparing myself to confront the local mafia, the chauffeurs or death himself holding a sharpened sickle on the other side. It was worse. One of the officers who raped me in the airport was standing in front of my apartment. I opened the door a crack and with no warning he served me my court documents and told me to come with him.

"Why?" I asked, incredulously.

"Because with your fake passport you are now considered a partner in crime along with the traffickers. They're going to trial in two weeks and you will need to be there to prove your innocence."

"But you found the diary with all the evidence," I responded. "Haven't I been cleared?"

"Not yet." He said, walking towards the elevator and dragging me with him.

I didn't trust him but he still carried that unflappable authority peculiar to law officers, so, I acquiesced. He talked sporadically on his phone for the majority of the drive, a drive that took me far from my home and closer to the airport. Disoriented, I had no idea where we were when he slowly pulled into a car park in front of a residential complex.

"Where are we?" I asked him. "What are we doing here?"

The air tasted grey and the stress of so many unknowns brought my fever back. I wouldn't even know how to get home from here on the transit system, I thought, looking at the damp ground below my tired feet. We went upstairs into a room that I assumed was his. It had one bed, a well-used looking bed sheet and the same stench of generic cleanser and human despair that I had come to know far too well in Toronto motel rooms.

I knew what was coming, and I didn't fight him. I knew the knife edge I was walking on and so did he. This was a man who was abusing his authority and I was helplessly objectified once again. I whimpered dejectedly as he took his clothes off and pushed my head onto his member, praying that he would come to his senses and stop this before it went any further. But he didn't, he just hammered my head down like a gavel atop a judge's bench and tossed me on the bed like a lifeless mannequin who had been designed for degradation.

He violated me on top, from behind and in every other position imaginable. I was lifeless. I thought to myself, "You piece of crap. If this makes you feel like a big man go for it, you heartless, two-faced crooked piece of crap."

For the very first time throughout this harrowing experience, I became visibly angry, but mostly with myself. "This is my fault. I provoked this. I should never have gotten into his car. I am a dirty whore. I deserve this," I thought.

After an hour it was over. He tried to kiss me, but I pulled away telling him he wasn't my boyfriend. With that, he ordered me to get dressed and get the hell out. "I'm done with you!" he barked. I felt like a cheap whore and worse yet, like garbage kicked to the curb. I found myself stranded and freezing at midnight in the middle of nowhere. I had no idea where I was, nor did I have any money to get home. Exhausted and still sick with fever and chills, I made my way to a bus stop and leaned my head against the wall in desperation. A bus rolled up forty minutes later, so I asked the driver how I might get to my neighborhood. In Hungary, we don't pay upfront when using mass transit. Transit officials make random checks for passes, and if you don't have one, they send you a pricey ticket in the mail. So it was a risk to ride without a pass, but I had to get home.

I sleepily walked into my apartment that morning. My brother didn't wake up and I feverishly popped two pills and combed my hair until my scalp hurt. I then made my way into my bedroom and willed the world away. Tucking myself in, I tried to sleep.

Chapter 9

I awoke to the sound of knocking at my apartment door in mid-day. My brother had long since gone to work, and I had barely slept off the trauma associated with my previous official visitor, so I was naturally terrified by the sound. I doused my face with a quick splash of water and tiptoed out into the hall to take a peek. It was two men dressed officially. They didn't look like mafia and seemed immediately receptive and sensitive to how fearful I was. The taller of the two had warm blue eyes and spoke with the gentle tone of a new father.

"Hi, Ms. Nagy?"

"Yes?" I tentatively replied.

"My name is Miklos Feher, and this is my partner Officer Dudas. We're from the National Police Organized Crime Department. Are you busy?" he asked.

"I'm only getting out of bed. What can I do for you?" I replied.

"Well, we want you to come with us. It's not mandatory but we'd like to ask you some questions about a wanted man named Sasha. Do you know him?"

These men were trained to read peoples reactions, so they knew that I was familiar with Sasha before I had even begun to speak.

Excusing myself to my room, I got dressed, brushed my teeth and looked out my bedroom window for suspicious cars in the parking lot. If the traffickers were watching me now, seeing me leave with two police officers would surely have negative repercussions on me and my family, so on the way out I insisted that we be brisk.

We went downstairs and got into a car that was clearly an unmarked police vehicle. I ducked in quickly and must have been visibly uneasy in the backseat because Feher began speaking to ease the air. "So we've received your statement from our guys at the airport and we'd like to hear more about the agency that recruited you," he said. "But most of all, what can you tell us about this Sasha character who you mentioned in your report?"

"Honestly, I really don't think that this guy exists," I said. "I never saw him and I never actually saw the Hungarians talking to him on the phone either. It was just lots of stories. I think the guys in Canada who drove the girls around just made the stories up to scare us."

"Don't be alarmed Ms. Nagy," Feher said evenly. "But Sasha does exist and we've been investigating his ring of smugglers, pimps, traffickers murderers and gun runners for almost eight years now. They're on Europe's most wanted list and they are very dangerous. We're hoping you can tell us everything you can possibly remember about Sasha and the stories you've heard about him."

I began to shake as I remembered grisly details from our 'cautionary tales' and was confronted with the fact that they may have been true. The stories about him were so brutal, I recalled. I could have sworn that he was only a tool used for brainwashing us.

Is this the same Sasha that murdered a girl with a baseball bat and left her to die in front of a farm in Germany? Or the same Sasha that set fire to an eighteen year old brunette in a Bulgarian garage? Stuttering for a moment, I replied that it sounded like him.

"Could you testify against him, Timea?" he asked with noticeable trepidation. "Think of how many more girls would be spared. Who knows how many more lives it could save?"

"What about my life? You know that he will find someone to kill me or do it himself. How will you protect me?" I asked.

Feher was silent for a moment. "The witness protection program in Hungary isn't anything we're proud of, Timea. You would have to understand, as we do, the sacrifices you'd be making by doing this for us."

"I'd have to hide for the rest of my life, officer. I'd never be the same again."

We continued doing laps around my immediate neighborhood in the thick silence of the unmarked car. Finally, we stopped in front of my building. Feher gave me his card and asked me to call him if and when I wanted to testify. I took the card and thanked them for driving me home. I was quietly grateful that I hadn't been raped a third time by an officer of the law.

I rushed into my apartment complex struggling to suppress images of my own brutal murder at the hands of

Sasha from creeping into my mind. In the elevator with the doors slowly closing, I pressed the button to hurry the process up. No one was in the lobby but I tapped out a frantic beat until the door finally shut. Could I live like this, knowing that people like him existed? And that they could reach me or my family at any time they chose?

I didn't breathe in the hallway and focused exclusively on locking my door as soon as I was able. I lit a cigarette in my room. One after another I smoked them to their filters, watching the parking lot grow darker as night fell. My eyes were so fixed on the idea of finding movement that in the depths of paranoia, they may have created some. I chain-smoked and obsessed for days in a similar fashion. It was clear after four days of feeding a fever with cigarette smoke, that I could not go on like this.

Living beyond social borders is not living. One must escape fear, and unlike the 'learned helplessness' that one learns in the cloudy terror which encompasses the mind of a Stockholm syndrome victim, I began to consider fleeing again rather then staying to fight the local police and Europe's mafia. That night my brother burst into my room, beckoning me to follow him to the living room.

"Wow Timea, someone must be in big trouble," he began excitedly. "Come see the north side."

We followed each other like kids to the north window and stared out into the parking lot. "See the white one?" he asked.

"Yeah." I answered.

"With the paint job?" he continued.

"Yeah." I answered again.

"It's a cop in the middle of a stakeout," he stated with an air of satisfaction.

"Oh." I muttered, recognizing it.

"Follow me to the south window."

I followed him to a window in the living room where he was pointing to a Mercedes with tinted windows.

"That's the mafia staking someone out themselves," he announced.

At that moment, both the police and mafia appeared to me clearly for the first time since my return from Toronto. Days passed and although I was tired I couldn't fall sleep. My fever worsened. Confusion and paranoia became my norm. I didn't do laundry or dishes. My brother often forgot that I was home and so did I.

I became less careful about managing the symptoms of my depression and I stopped eating. I shook nervously and drank black tea. I chain smoked and helplessly ran back and forth between the north and south windows of our apartment, watching my watchers with obsessive compulsion. My thoughts turned, predictably, to escape.

I would go to England, instead of Canada. No. Just out of Hungary. To be anywhere but inside this routine where I felt like a martyr every time I left the house for toilet paper would be an improvement. In Canada I could get a job right away and even find a place to stay. But how would I get through customs? I wasn't allowed to go back to Canada for twelve months. I feverishly plotted escape plans and hastily redrew them every time I hit a logistical wall.

As my escape plans grew more wild and speculative, I began to realize that for any of my plans to work, I needed a passport. I remembered Feher telling me that none of the charges were in the system yet and that this meant I could still apply for a passport. I needed to leave my apartment without being detected, first, however.

I remembered one summer not long before, when I'd gone sunbathing on the roof of our building. After an hour or so when I tried to return inside, I'd been locked out and thus stranded on the roof, or so I thought. I wandered around the roof looking for alternate routes off when I found a second staircase at the opposite end. This proceeded to take me to another elevator which descended down to the most concealed of all three entrances to our apartment complex.

That evening at midnight, I dressed myself and went to the roof, re-enacting my sunbathing scenario. It had been a while since my soul had been moved by anything other than fear or shame, but when that second door swung open under the constellations over Budapest, I was infused with joy and a newfound faith in myself. For the first time in a long time, I was a woman with a plan.

Half-asleep I bolted up as my brother closed the door behind him on his way to work. I hopped into my pants, applied some makeup, shook my head at the fatigued stranger in the mirror staring back at me, and I was off to the passport office.

As I boarded the Monday morning train headed towards central Budapest, my mind raced as I recalled logistics from my first application for work in Canada and I made rapid calculations, searching amongst a myriad of probable outcomes for any glimmer of hope. I recalled suspicious people, planned dates of arrival and departure, considered deadlines, red tape, the law, morality, the ego, the id, ethics and questions of identity. Even if I was refused entry to Canada, I still had to leave Hungary, and soon. In my chaotic mental world of narrowing choices and battered self-esteem, purgatory was an improvement over hell. I bit my nails when strangers glanced at me and began to worry about what I looked like to these blasé commuters as I muttered unintelligibly to myself.

I finally made it to the passport office and talked to the first available attendant. There was a more expensive rapid procedure available to me that promised me new documentation in only three business days. So, theoretically, I'd get my passport by Thursday and could be on a flight any time after that. I calmly asked her if I would be renewing the same passport number and she informed me that I would actually be receiving a new number, taking a new photo and getting an entirely new passport.

My next stop was the travel agency. Narrowing down my departure dates, I decided that Monday or Tuesday on the following week would work best. If I could evade the statues in the Mercedes as well as the crooked cops who raped me, I'd be long gone before they came to wrestle me into the courtroom to testify against Sasha and the Hungarian mafia on the following Friday.

The travel agent told me with outlandish kindness that the only day I could fly out would be this Friday, the very day after I was supposed to receive my new passport. The next flight would be two weeks from now on the day after my court date. It was too close for comfort. What if I bought the ticket for the first flight and I didn't get my passport on time? I squirmed and excused myself for a cigarette. Returning after only half of it, I said a quiet prayer and booked my flight for the coming Friday at six a.m.

Chapter 10

I returned home, nervous and hopeful about my impending departure. I conducted my now habitual inspection of the parking lot, and I noticed that the Mercedes had disappeared from the south window but that the police car continued its ominous vigil on the north side. I sat at home and tried to figure out what to tell my mom and brother. I called Christine in Canada and told her that I had a ticket back. "Are you serious?" she asked.

Even though the specifics of my arrival were tentative at best, I imagined her eyes, beaming happily at me, as I strolled out from the arrival doors at the airport. We agreed that she'd pick me up. And as I hung up the phone the oddest thing happened. It didn't stop ringing. For the remainder of the night, I stayed in my bedroom awake to the constant jangling of the phone with my pillow wrapped tightly around my head.

Hungary wasn't equipped with call display or answering machines, so I let the insanity of bell-to-bell-to-bell-to-bell vibrations persist long into the night until I called my mom just to silence it.

We hadn't talked much since I had been home because I was entirely too ashamed of what had happened to me in Canada. And, like most daughters, I had an impossible time lying to my mother. If she asked what I did, I would tell her. Giving my burdens to someone else wasn't a possibility, especially my beloved Mama. On the phone I told her I was leaving, once again.

"What? I've yet to see you and you're leaving again?" she exclaimed.

"Yes, Mama," I said, knowing that if I made it to Canada successfully, I wouldn't be returning to see her for a long time.

"Well, when's your flight? I'm coming to the airport to see you off," she announced.

"Mama, please, I'll be back in a few more months," I evaded, not wanting her to bare witness to her only daughter being refused or arrested or worse at the airport.

She persisted. "Timea, I'll be there, shush now. What time are you leaving?" she persisted.

"Mama, please." I returned abruptly, ending our conversation.

Hastily, I hung up the phone. It then rang twice and stopped. Then the ringing began again and didn't stop that afternoon or evening. Long into the night it continued, conveying a not so subtle threat from either the police or mafia. To this day, I don't know if the police or the mafia were responsible for the harassment, and, frankly, at this point it didn't matter. I wanted out. On the trip to the post office Tuesday morning, for a premature check for my passport, I took a circuitous route home, welcoming the chance for some fresh air and some additional stealth.

The detour led me past churches and housing rather then people on bicycles and busy streets humming with traffic, but I could still hear the cars and busses. I heard the commuter train that I had taken for twelve years screech into a station. My audio-periphery felt amplified and I became starkly aware of all the familiar things I was once again about to leave behind. To distract myself, I thought of my sweet cat, Filemon. He was my world and I only wished he could tag along with me on my upcoming journey.

He was just five months old when he followed me home five years ago. I remember hearing his little paws on the ground and seeing his distinctive blue eyes peer up at me from the sidewalk. They were his guide that day and I was so grateful that they directed his orange body towards me. He was collarless and followed me straight in the front door of my apartment and watched me carefully as I closed the elevator door. Mewing as the door opened at the eighth floor, he skipped over the gap and led me straight to my apartment. I thought it was such a miracle that he seemed to know which one was mine and also, miraculously, that my brother didn't put up a fight as he traipsed cockily inside.

From that day on he was my soul-mate. He would share my bed every night, and he was my companion when I was sick or depressed. During dark periods in my life, he would refuse food and water until my mood or health changed for the better. Later that day when my brother came home from work, I told him that once again I would be going back to Canada. "And soon," I said. I waited for another earful about my worth, or lack thereof. "Ok, Timea," he said with his slouching back turned. He surprised me with his nonchalant acceptance.

As children, he had always favored having the last word in any conversation. But like the one song you pass over on your favorite album, he had become indifferent to me now, almost to the point of ignoring me. I saw him accept that he would once again be earning rent alone. He conceded so fast it frightened me. Was this just the calm before a hailstorm of verbal abuse?

"Does Mama know?" he whispered.

"Yes," I replied quietly.

He kept his back to me and I stayed in my room for the rest of the evening. Morning came and I prepared to sneak out and make my way to the post office. My home phone had continued ringing constantly. Ever since I had received that threatening phone call from the agency during my last stint in Hungary, I had shut down my mobile as well. Considering the circumstances with my boyfriend and co-workers, I couldn't assume anyone else would be contacting me. I left the rooftop on my alternate route to the post office, past the churches, the statues of the eagles and the wide front lawns, in hopes that I wouldn't be tailed.

They should have at least sent the passport by now, I thought. Blocking out all the weather and lively sounds of my walk was the sound of my home phone still ringing ominously in my head. I entered the post office and the woman at the counter shook her head, stopping me in my tracks. No passport yet. Two days until my flight was ready to depart. Dejectedly, I thanked her and made my way back out into the street.

For reasons unknown I became keenly aware of the stone detailing on the church facades during my walk home. They gave me pause on my empty handed walk home and thawed my dejection with the sweet smell of incense. For the first time in my life, I walked inside. Moving past the holy water and cross strewn pews of the back row, I sat up front where I instantly broke down into tears. I needed sanctuary. I cried so hard it echoed off the high wood walls and came back to me like someone else's voice, momentarily startling me out of the fit. Then a real hand touched my shoulder.

Had the Mafia tailed me, following me in here? To my relief I looked into the clean shaven face of the local minister. Apparently I'd been crying so hard that he had heard me in his office, buried all the way in the back wing of the church. I was so embarrassed that I began apologizing spastically. He quickly stopped me and sat down, asking if I'd like to talk. Softly, I started crying again, but this time I couldn't stop. I covered my face with my hands and felt him put his arm across my shoulders, rocking back and forth, whispering words I couldn't make out until my tears were spent. In the silence of the church, he once again asked if I wanted to talk.

"Yes, Father," I said. "I do want to get something off my chest."

All I had wanted since I'd returned to Hungary was one naked moment of unrestrained verbal release. But nothing came; it choked in my throat and I started crying again. All the frustration, emotional strain and tangled nerves, that so desperately needed the healing balm of serenity, rained down on his vestments. I couldn't talk intelligibly, so I left, embarrassed, after excusing myself.

I made it back into my apartment and was pleasantly surprised to find that neither the police car nor the Mercedes were stalking one another, me, or anyone else from my parking lot. The telephone had stopped its incessant ringing and all I could do was wait out the evening with Filemon on my lap and torture myself with all the variables that jeopardized my plan. My plane left in thirty hours and I still did not have a passport. My strained nerves were beginning to snap under constant strain and tension.

As morning broke on the day before my departure, I begun packing and checked off some errands to kill time. I wanted to give the postman every available moment of his business day to drop my package off, so I busied myself until just before closing time.

I made a final call to my Mama, wrote a letter to my brother and held Filemon as often as I could. For hours that day my eyes were puffy from tears and I noticed that dark circles were beginning to appear beneath them, significantly aging my youthful complexion.

I prodded my face in the mirror until 4:30 p.m. when I walked out the front door for what was, hopefully, my final walk to the post office. They closed at 5 p.m., so I knew if the passport was coming today, it would be there now. Entering pensively I saw the same woman behind the counter, busy with a line that snaked halfway around the room. She was tending to everyone herself. As if sensing me coming in, she quickly looked up and into my eyes, recognizing me in an instant. She shook her head negatively to save me waiting in line to hear the bad news.

All I could think was, "I am done, over. My nine lives have been exhausted and I won't make that plane tomorrow."

I fled to the church again and I absolutely lost myself. Lying on the front pew, damning the absence of God, hurling blasphemy after blasphemy. I prayed that I would be crushed by a ceiling fan or struck by lighting. Between gasping sobs I clenched my fists and weakly punched my temples. I fell to the floor before the red carpeted stairs and started crying again. I remember that feeling. I was shaking, everything was grey, I didn't see a way out. Once again, the soft spoken minister approached me from his office, smelling reassuringly like eucalyptus wood. He lifted me up and held me.

"I think it's time we talked, child" he said kindly. "What has forsaken you so? Can you not see that you're safe in this, the bosom of the Lord?" he asked.

I backed out of his arms and asked boldly, "Where is God, Father? Where is He? My life depends on a few very basic and very important things, all of which I have been praying for. But God remains silent. No, He remains cruel and invisible, a passive observer of the chaotic world He should never have created. He has turned His back on us while we scream sounds that He, seemingly, doesn't have the capacity to hear."

I buried my head in my hands while the minister began rubbing my shoulders calmly. "What very important things do you need to live today?" He began. "Do you have a warm home, fresh air and food in your refrigerator? These are God's gifts to you, the rest only you can decide to need or not need. It is not God's responsibility to make your mind up for you or give you the ambition and knowledge to make money to pay your bills."

He had assumed that I was simply poor and sad, so I spilled everything. "I need my passport to get on a flight and leave tomorrow. It's a very important flight that I can't miss or else me and my family are dead and the post office didn't receive it when they said they would." I blurted.

"You said the post office?" he queried.

"Yes" I answered.

"Did you think to check your mailbox at home first? They changed the system two months ago. How long have you lived here in Budapest?"

My heart stopped and so did my tears. Except for this day, I'd been leaving my building from the roof top, so I hadn't even thought to check my mailbox in the main lobby. I thanked him profusely and raced out the door, my pace increasing until I walked in the main entrance of my building towards my mailbox. My hands trembled as I found the right key and opened the box. There in a white envelope, waiting patiently, was my shiny new passport, with my real name on it this time. I had so much energy that I bounded up to the eighth floor, forgoing the elevator. This was better than any Christmas morning I had ever experienced.

I flung open the front door and feverishly packed up the last of my belongings - the widest and most yawning mug in my collection as well as clothes and old photos of my mother, father and brother. While I was busy packing, Filemon made a nest piece by piece on top of my rapidly filling suitcase and it appeared that he wasn't going to move.

If he was a man I'd have married him in an instant. Having to leave him for the third time was heart wrenching. At two in the morning, I shut my eyes to steal some sleep. I awoke abruptly again at four and I kissed my brother in his sleep, and laid my written words beside him like a departing lover. He didn't wake up. "How many times can one woman be born?" I wondered, hustling towards the taxi station with my suitcase. The morning birds sang me into an awaiting cab while the driver stuffed my suitcase into the trunk with a slam.

As we drove towards the airport, police sirens overwhelmed bird songs and terrified me as they sped past us in the ascending dawn sun. I sunk lower and lower into my seat with my hand on my passport like a bar of gold, making inane small talk with the gruff cabbie smoking placidly. We finally arrived at my terminal, and with a mediocre tip to the driver, I was off. I had very little money left and I needed everything I had in order to survive until I saw Christine again in Toronto. The departures area was crawling with officers and I knew that visible sleep deprivation and fear made me an object of interest, if not outright suspicion in their eyes.

"Timea, Timea!" I heard, incredibly, seemingly coming out of nowhere. Suddenly, my compact Hungarian mother heeled up behind me and gave me a squeeze. I cringed. "Mama? What are you doing here? I told you I hated long good-byes" I blurted.

"Yes, but I had to see my little girl at least once before she left to explore the world," she playfully responded. "When I was a little girl, we were working every day for our bed and supper on a day to day basis! Things were much simpler then: family, health…"

I persuaded her to follow me outside for a cigarette and told her nicely that she should just go home. She kissed me with tears that came on like a faucet. I understood what she was feeling, but I had to put her on the next bus that pulled up to the curb. She had dressed up to see me off and looked lovely. I told her so and also noted how much her lavender perfume seemed to lift her spirits. We hugged like old friends and I waved to her while she peered back at me sadly. I could see her asking a stranger if the seat beside him was taken while the bus pulled away.

My next hurdle was the passport check. A week ago, the detectives told me that my case wasn't in the system yet, so I wouldn't be flagged as having a record. But that was a week ago. I got in line and concerned myself only with looking normal, which I can say now, probably left me looking the exact opposite. No one in front or behind me could conceive of how loudly I was praying in my head. Miraculously managing to fake a smile, I was flustered by the sudden onset of a panic attack. I remembered what the two officers did to me the first time around and felt flashes of pain throughout my body as I approached the window. The officer opened my passport, scanned it, looked into the system, looked at me, looked back at the passport, closed my passport and handed it back to me as he looked over my shoulder, beckoning the next passenger. "Next!" he bellowed.

My relief was strong enough to threaten my studied facade, so I forced myself to stride away from the booth with a gait somewhere between a sleepwalker's and a holiday shopper's. I continued this way until I reached a long escalator that would take me to the bag check. Half way up the slow escalator, I was startled to see a woman waiting at the top in an Air Canada uniform. One at a time she spoke to the folks ahead of me. Each of them did a few confused circles around her before getting back onto the escalator down towards the exit.

Why were they leaving? What was wrong with the process? "Hello Ma'am, what's your destination today?" the Air Canada representative asked.

"I'm going from here to London and then on to Toronto," I replied.

"I'm sorry Miss, but Air Canada is on strike as of today," she replied. She was very sincere, but it didn't help. "Unfortunately there will be no planes going to Toronto until it's resolved."

"Excuse me?" I asked flatly.

She repeated. "Can you stay in Budapest for another day or two?"

In spite of myself, I laughed. "No, that's not a possibility. I have no choice but to be on a plane today."

"It's only going to London ma'am, so unfortunately you won't make it to Toronto as planned," she continued. "However if you choose to go to London, you can stay there until the strike is resolved."

What she didn't know was that after paying for urgent express service on my new passport, buying a last minute plane ticket and taking the taxi here, I was left nothing but a handful of change in my pocket which had to last me until I got to Canada. "Of course that's no problem, as long as I'm on the plane to London I can make do once I get there." Panhandling, begging or worse - whatever – "Just get me out of Hungary", I thought as she showed me to the check-in counter.

After dropping off some of the little baggage I had, I bounded straight for the bathroom and stayed there until we got the call to board the plane. I was truly on the run, and the eyes and the skin on my face were beginning to look like I had been for years. Hungary was behind me now and Canada lay ahead. Escaping was taking its toll on my appearance so I put on some makeup to create a more stable visage for my trip.

People walked in and out of the bathroom as I took all the face time I needed: young girls, business women, mothers towing whining daughters and the occasional mistaken man entered and left around me. I felt like a statue in the middle of a flourishing afternoon park but quickly snapped out of it. We were about to take off, so I made my way to the gate and onto an awaiting aircraft. I closed my eyes and thought about Filemon until we were in the air. For the third time in only four months, I felt a plane heave into the sky and watched carefully as we took the initial stomach lurching lap around the city.

I looked down and saw the estranged motherland I had just exiled myself from and no amount of churches, history, traditions or culture could pay back what the people inside its borders had done to my wide-eyed optimism and youthful innocence. "Never again!" I thought confidently as we made our way towards the lights of Paris and London, I was gone.

Chapter 11

I awoke to the sound of our landing gear hitting the tarmac at London Heathrow, and I listened to the metallic clicks that other riders made as they preemptively released their seat-belts and pawed at their luggage in the overhead bins. We weren't at our gate yet, and I wasn't in the same rush as the people around me. I was relieved to be out of Budapest, as to what lay beyond that, I hadn't really had time to think about it as yet.

Imprisoned at the airport until the strike was cleared up, I was prepared to fast while everyone else hurried themselves back into their well scheduled and compartmentalized lives. Who could blame them? White Europeans in this day and age are some of the most inherently fortunate people to have walked this planet and many have little time for the tribulations of others. I waited until the last passenger had their things and filed in like a drone behind them.

Congregating just outside the gate was one of the angriest and most vocal mobs of travelers I'd ever seen. It was chaotic. Families, white and blue collar workers, sport teams in uniform, foreigners en route, backpacking students and restless goths; all were being arranged into perturbed groups who hounded their corresponding Air Canada representative. At this point my English was still so poor that I could only watch and wonder. To me, they looked like little groups being individually preached to by well mannered staff who corralled the people from atop makeshift podiums.

Slowly but surely, the groups were calmed down, and they retreated to shuttle buses with their Air Canada reps. I wandered aimlessly through the chaos, taking fake perusals of food I couldn't afford and getting hungrier by the lap.

I had no idea where they went but I welcomed the change in volume, so I made a little nest with my bags in the corner and put my head down to take a nap. As anyone who has been truly broke knows, it can be hard to sleep on an empty stomach. But after a few long and restless hours, I had the gate to myself and began to drift into sleep. A woman woke me with the brisk clacking of her shoes. She was walking straight toward me and I rose from the floor to meet her.

She asked me something I didn't understand and looked at the stickers on my bags, pointing to the Air Canada logo. She mimed for me to follow her, so I collected my things and was led through the expansive airport to a waiting shuttle bus full of anxious looking passengers. She told me the name of a hotel until she was sure I understood it and was gone as fast she came, back into the airport like a firefighter at work.

We drove away from the airport and into the cookie-cutter pseudo subdivision of hotels that surround airports. Stopping at luxurious hotel after luxurious hotel, at some forty second intervals between them, the driver eventually pointed to me. After a half dozen people had gone, I exited to the rain-soaked street, led by a bowing man into an elegant crystal laden lobby with bright white lighting.

I went straight to the front desk and instinctively handed over my boarding pass. The clerk scanned it, didn't ask for any form of payment or show me any receipts but smiled and handed over a plastic credit card. She grabbed an imaginary door knob with her right hand and inserted the card into a mock door with her left. I understood and wondered how I got so lucky despite everything that had happened? Air Canada had never seen an inconvenienced customer as grateful as I was. Even the slightest hint of security illuminated me. And just as I began to thank providence for my good fortune, she handed me three tickets for the buffet in the first floor dining hall.

After eating until I couldn't eat anymore, I eased into my small but elegantly furnished hotel room. I lifted the covers off the foot of the bed, and got myself ready to enjoy this experience. With no immediate danger and being free from threats, I called my Mama.

I told her about my hotel and the reason for my short stay in London, but I had to keep the conversation short. How much would this call be costing the airline? The free buffet was priceless enough, and my mother herself had taught me not to abuse the charity of others. I knew she would understand, when we parted, she sounded happy to have heard my voice.

I took a shower and turned the TV on. I padded around the room while the news spoke about some story that was practically and linguistically meaningless to me. I thought about what tomorrow might bring as I wiggled my toes under pristine white sheets and opened expansive French windows for some fresh air. I felt safe and secure and ready to sleep, even though I knew from experience that luxuries like the cleanliness and quiet this room afforded me would be temporary.

At six in the morning, my phone rang. Rolling over, I lifted the receiver to my ear and heard an automatic message that repeated itself. I didn't understand it but heard nothing terribly concerning, so I went back to sleep. I slept until eleven when I made my way downstairs, eagerly anticipating a strong black coffee as my first course at the buffet.

As I entered a ghostly vacant dining hall, I heard a tap dancer approaching me from behind. Hurriedly, the woman from the front desk began speaking over my head. I couldn't catch much and motioned for her to slow down. I had control of maybe twenty percent of the sensibly sped English language, but the quickening that came with urgency or a new accent would throw me off every time. I wondered what she was talking about. I also wondered why people who are attempting to communicate across a language barrier also assume that 'louder' equals 'easier to understand.'

She quickly moved onto miming and opened her arms wide to describe a vast wingspan. "Flight?" I offered. She nodded, tapping her watch, pointing behind her back, looking me in the eyes and making an unmistakable X with her index fingers in front of her throat. She faced me quizzically to make sure I understood. I had missed the flight and the strike was over. I pointed to the ground, trying to sign "now" and then used my other hand's pointer finger to leap frog over it. I made a pensive okay sign, shrugging my shoulders hopefully. Could she understand this charade?
"Tomorrow, okay?" she replied. And pointed to the six on her watch. If I had understood correctly, I was on my way to Toronto tomorrow morning at six.

I called Christine from my room to pass the time and practice my English. I found myself whispering as though I suspected the phone was tapped. Christine coached me on how to act when I got to Canadian Customs, what to say and how to look and sound like a real visitor. "Never been before! Visitor, visitor? and smile, smile Timea! - CN Tower and big waterfall visitor! and laugh like the customs agent is your best friend. Tap your purse, tap tap tap your purse!" she instructed.

She was a helpful coach and wanted what was best for me, always making sure I was comfortable and confident with my actions. I bid her farewell and rested my eyes for an afternoon catnap. I awoke to the sound of the phone ringing at six a.m. waking me for my dash to the airport.

I wasn't missing this plane for anything, so foregoing makeup I jumped on the elevator and made my way into the lobby as quickly as possible. I was still rubbing small bits of sleep out of my eyes as I made my way to a large group of fellow travelers. With my luggage and tickets in hand, I followed them to the shuttle, the gate and eventually onto the airplane itself.

They didn't name a tea after London fog because the fog wasn't memorable, and this flight was memorable for all the wrong reasons. The fog above London seems endlessly thick when you're on a multi passenger jet trying to fly through it. Turbulence abounded and bounced the aircraft around for the entire eight hour and twenty minute flight. God willing, we eventually touched down. We had made it. A number of passengers put their hands together when we hit the tarmac and I clapped right along with them.

While everyone around me was happy and excited to arrive in Toronto I began to feel apprehensive about my impending customs and immigration interview. I remembered what Christine had said to me about being strictly a visitor. Name landmarks and smile like you have nothing to hide. In my favor, the airport's security and customs processes were chaotic in the aftermath of the strike. Lineups were two to three times longer than normal with the weather and regular baggage issues. I hoped that the agents wouldn't be checking everyone with their regular fervor.

I approached the lineups and panned quickly across the agent's faces. Who had the latest night last night, or was having the worst day today? Which one looked like a parent? Who was the most addicted to their job? Who would make or break my life? This was the final hurdle between me and a life free of terror. I wanted to get it right. My eyes stopped and came back to a Caucasian lady in the middle. She was blond, in her mid-forties and wearing a long pony tail. I noticed her crack a smile at the arriving traveler who had just left her booth so I hustled into her stream of impatient passengers. I stepped up to the counter and started smiling. I gave her my passport and the invitation letter I had received from Christine saying that she planned to take me to Niagara Falls, the CN Tower, surrounding casinos and so forth.

All she asked me about was Niagara Falls. I smiled and said, "Yes, Niagara, yes!"
She swiped my passport, looked at the computer and back to me. She picked up a red marker, put something on the first page and gave me my passport back, motioning that I should continue past her. As I walked towards the exit, I fell in behind a family of four who were being directed into a secondary investigation room by a customs agent. He had reviewed the markings on their father's passport in red and sent them all in together.

I began to wonder if that was the fate which awaited me. All of a sudden, I felt as though everything had slipped into slow motion. I could see the automatic doors opening and closing a few meters ahead. I could see the excited faces beyond the door, people waiting for loved ones straining to catch that first glimpse of a returning loved one. I mustered my courage and stepped up to the next available officer and handed over my passport. In one fluid motion, he gazed at it, closed it and pointed to the open door ahead.

A welcome wave of relief washed over me. Yes! I had made it! The crisp scent of clean Canadian air hit my nose before I had a chance to register what had happened. I must have looked like a newborn baby with my head facing the crowd as I began scanning, looking for Christine. I kept looking around until I saw the familiar blond hair and elegant outfit. We hugged and I didn't take my arms from around her neck until we walked out of the airport and I got down to kiss the ground. I know that Christine was embarrassed, but I didn't care. I kissed the dirty ground at Pearson Airport. Canada was terra firma to me, sacred earth, and nothing could have appeared cleaner to me at that moment.

It was six twenty three pm on September 4th,, 1998, when I finally arrived back in Toronto. This was my third time crossing the border in four months and I was almost positive it would be the last for a very long time.

Chapter 12

For my first month back in Canada, I stayed at Christine's house in Scarborough. She lived in the same house with her husband of four years. I felt like a Hungarian girl trying to slowly learn the language of day-to-day Canadian life. I did small chores like washing dishes and cooking meals, but Christine knew that I didn't really have a plan. I had only a visitor's visa that would expire in 6 months, so any money I made would have to be made under the table.

As terrible as it was and only after some heart-wrenching soul searching, I swallowed my pride and decided to dance. It was the only thing that I knew I could do under the table, and there was a club in North York that Christine knew of where I could work on occasion and make my own hours. "No stress" she said. I didn't have the faculty to communicate the fact that for me, there would always be stress associated with dancing, but I needed the money. The club was called the Red Rose, and was my only viable option at the time. Christine's husband also offered to drive me there when I needed, and he mentioned that we should go have a look at it first, to make sure it suited me before committing.

Owned by a straight talking, cigar smoking Russian ex-KGB agent named Alex, the club was the cleanest place in the area, in regards to clientele and staff. Alex monitored it all. He had cameras in every corner, and was notorious for showing problem clients his office with the snap of his fingers. The sight of his military hair cut was enough to keep my back upright and straight as a broom stick. His near obsessive attention to detail meant that no cops or immigration officers would be poking around looking for work permits and really, because Christine had recommended it, how bad could it be?

Meeting Alex was intimidating but only because I knew about his past. He remained as unassuming as one could be while wearing a crisp Armani suit and a loud Rolex which screamed for attention. He listened patiently and with demonstrable empathy and concern, folded his fingers on top of his desk and encouraged me to go on with my story about how I had made my way across the world and into his club.

I started work slowly - only a few times a week to contribute fairly to the rent and to cover my share of the groceries. But Alex noticed something in me and began hinting to me that I could work more if I liked. "How often do you do coke?" he bluntly asked me, one day.

"Excuse me Alex? Smoke? Not too often."

"No, Timtim, cocaine." He responded, "Or drink for that matter?"

"Oh, the last thing on my mind is a party," I confessed. "I'm worried about eating and sleeping in a warm bed, that's all."

"You're a sight for sore eyes Timea," he smiled warmly. "And one in a million in this business. Whenever you need anything, you let me know, OK?"

I agreed to work the day shifts and started around noon each day reasoning that it would be safer to finish before seven p.m. and there would be less chance of a surprise raid by immigration during those hours. Do one stage show every hour for fifty dollars plus tips a day, talk to customers for a little free English lesson here and there, and pray that I could find a legitimate work visa on the floor of a cab or tacked to my locker in the next six months.

Long quiet days turned into endless weeks and I had a disturbing thought: My life wasn't much different from my time under the "protection" of the coercive Hungarians. The only difference was that I was free. But not free from boredom. What was freedom, I wondered? I worked during the day and went to Christine's house for dinner at night.

I had no one to talk to and felt like my candle was burning out in a dark strip joint every afternoon. The stage was my cell, my cubicle, and sometimes I looked forward to the exercise, expression of the dance and the adrenaline. Things became very askew and my morals felt like abstract ethical wreckage. Unsure of my motivations or priorities, I became a shadow of someone I used to know. Sometimes I would try to make small talk with the bartenders or the waitresses, but they weren't always interested in being my English teacher, so I stopped burdening them, too.

Scarborough was about an hour and a half away from the club and was accessible by the subway and the bus. Aching for direction, I decided to stop getting rides to work and to try the commute on public transit by myself. During my first few attempts, getting almost comically lost, I eventually found my way. I had given myself a chance for a small taste of adventure and spontaneity and it invigorated me. It was here that I finally got to see real Canadian people - every day working people on the subway who don't think about who's hunting them or strangers waiting for you to take your clothes off. These were fortunate people who simply get their morning coffee and read the newspaper with health cards and credit cards adorning their wallets. They belonged to someone. They belonged to a country. They had friends, family and pets to go home to. They had barbecues on the weekend, birthdays coming up, someone to call if they had a rough day, and people calling them just to say hi.

I had been working as a dancer for about a month or so when I eventually called my mom to tell her how I was doing. I dissembled and told her I was working in a Russian restaurant as a waitress. One Friday afternoon, Alex called me into his office and asked me if I could stay for the evening and help him out on the bar. A shooter girl had called in sick and he needed someone to cover her on the busiest night of the week. All I had to do was walk around and sell drinks. If the whole tray was bought, I made sixty dollars. I was so happy to finally get to do something other than dancing, so I said yes immediately.

That night, after selling the first tray in twenty minutes, Alex and the bar manager, Tamara, quickly refilled my tray over and over, another four times before the night was through. It was the most money I'd made with my clothes on in Canada, ever! At the end of the night Alex asked me if I wanted to do this every Friday night, and although I knew it was risky, I agreed. It was my first step in the direction of gaining straight work experience. The next Friday, I showed up to sell shooters again but was surprised when Tamara handed me a white top with black pants and said she wanted to train me to sell the whole beer and wine list. I wasn't the most confident bartender, learning the whole computer system in English and memorizing ten different beer names in a foreign language was daunting for me.

The first night, I made one hundred and twenty dollars in tips. This was a fortune to me, yet I still worked in fear of being found out by immigration. So, Alex, the Friday night DJ (a young kid with big plastic circles in his earlobes) and I all devised a plan. If undercover officers entered the building, the DJ would announce over the system that rain and showers were in the forecast, and I'd be out the back door before a drip hit the ground. I continued dancing for sleepy perverts during the day and learning the waitress ropes each Friday night. I would show up very early to help with odd chores because I was bored in the daytime and hoped that Alex would take me off the dancing shifts altogether.

One day I got to work early and Alex told me that a gentleman was waiting for me by a quiet table in the back. Not knowing anyone in this country, I asked Alex how the man said he knew me. Alex said the man wanted to help me, to which I doubtfully replied, "Really?"

"Don't worry," he assured me. "Just call me if you need anything."

I took three red carpeted steps down, made a right into the corner where he was sitting and said hello in Hungarian, to which the thin ailing man replied with confident fluency and the gnashing of silver teeth. He appeared to be in his sixties and said that he was working with other Hungarians 'in the business' and he wanted to talk to me about something he heard from another bartender last night. "She was very chatty," he finished, licking his gums with his grey-pink lips agape. "And told me the only Hungarian in the club didn't have status."

My first instinct was to signal Alex, but he continued.

"See, I can help you," he began. "We'll file papers for you as a refugee and you won't have to live in fear anymore. Do you live in fear now, Timea?" When he said my name, I stood up to leave, but he grabbed my wrist and looked me directly in the eyes. I could see liver spots on top of his head, scattered like moon craters in the black light of the club.

"I'll come back tomorrow and you're going to give me three hundred dollars to silence my loud mouth about your illegal status, and that's where we'll start." He reeked of desperation. "And then we're going to file you an application for refugee status which will be another twelve hundred dollars. Half of that you can pay me with lap dances this month."

"Don't…," I began.

"So, If I were you," he had two wet drops of spittle in the corners of his mouth that fizzled like beer foam when he spoke. "I wouldn't walk away so fast - I've been working with Immigration for ten years and have helped lots of girls to stay. Don't you want to stay, pumpkin?" This last word created more spittle on his lips. I nodded that I did want to stay.

I told him to come back the next day for my passport, the three hundred dollar bribe and a lap dance. As he relaxed his fingers from my wrist, I turned away and walked straight into Alex's office. I entered to find him and Tamara in front of the security TVs, watching the Hungarian man slip out the front door confidently. Alex turned and nodded to me calmly, "Let him come back."

This Hungarian man, as I found out, was well-known in the Hungarian underworld. His entire occupation consisted of cowardly fear tactics and he had threatened many girls in the same way he did me. Alex told me that he used to walk into any Hungarian businesses he could find and spot the illegal new comers. He would then execute his well practiced and somehow effective charade that included the speech I'd heard. He made his living preying on people, and got his tired old sexual kicks the same way.

The next day around one in the afternoon, the man arrived like clockwork. Tamara winked from behind the bar as Alex met him at the front door like a bouncer would. He promptly ushered him into his office and the DJ turned up the music while I stayed hidden in a secluded booth.

The music was incredibly loud. It drowned everything out and for twenty minutes my eyes stayed locked on the office door. From time to time I heard the bass beat off time and it sounded like the music was skipping.

Suddenly the office door swung open and the old man walked out with his sweaty hair matted to his skull. Alex was double checking that his Rolex was still in order on his wrist inside the office and the old Hungarian slid his left foot slowly across the carpet as if it was lame. He found the exit without looking for me once and it was clear that Alex's intervention had been effective.

Summer turned into fall and fall turned into winter. I moved in with Tamara who rented a two story townhouse fifteen minutes from the club in Toronto's infamous Jane and Finch district. I frequently heard police sirens near the main intersection and I don't remember ever enjoying deep sleep while living in this area. Apparently, it was one of Toronto's most notorious neighborhoods for gun violence and gang activity, but I didn't know. Local knowledge was beyond my improving but still limited communication skills.

I'd been at the Red Rose for almost six months and worked my way from being a bottom rung performer to shooter girl, then waitress, then bartender, and finally head bartender. As my responsibilities increased, my English also improved.

Learning a second language was one of the main reasons I came to Canada in the very first place and here I was, I thought, conversing with patrons across the bar about what they loved and what they hated. I became a part time psychiatrist working behind that bar and I loved to see how differently people reacted to the different words I used.

But one November day I was in the shower preparing for my night shift when I heard the code phrase, "rain and showers are in the forecast." I had no time to grab my clothing and I ran down the hallway in a man's jacket and towel. I swung open the heavy fireproof door and without shoes, ran across the busy street to take shelter in a little Mediterranean restaurant. My feet were freezing but I knew I had to wait at least an hour before I could go back to the club, so I snuck into the bathroom and warmed my feet with the hand dryer, hoping no one would intrude.

Chapter 13

With an expired visa, illegal status and no health card or social insurance number to speak of, I was beginning to wonder how much longer I could go on. To the Canadian government I was non-existent and I couldn't obtain help from them if my life depended on it. One grey despairing day that December, Christine, who read the Toronto Sun religiously, told me that something was happening inside Toronto clubs. She showed me an article that I didn't fully understand so she read it out loud to me:

"The raids on the strip clubs in suburbs west of Toronto, are part of a special joint task force set up with the hope of curbing organized prostitution and the international recruitment of sex slaves into Canada.

After weeks of undercover work and police intelligence, officers have found the first shards of evidence that confirm the presence of an organized group of eastern European traffickers. They have been and are currently moving women from Eastern Europe to Toronto, and forcing them to work in such clubs as the Second Locomotion in Mississauga, Toronto's Million Dollar Saloon and the Cannonball in Brampton.

Hundreds of police officers descended on the three strip clubs in a large-scale raid last night in hopes of shutting down the trafficking and exploitation of foreign exotic dancers."

But the story didn't stop there. She continued reading about an interview with a Hungarian girl, who told the police that she was brought to Canada on a fake passport and was forced to work in a strip club/massage salon as a prostitute. She continued the interview, saying the police did not deport her like she was forced to believe. Instead they used her as a witness in the case against her traffickers and worked on getting her permanent status as a refugee.

I felt as though they had interviewed me without my knowledge. I was so excited to hear my story in the paper and although I felt bad for the girl, she gave me hope. If I took my story to the proper officers, I could both attain status and legitimacy in the eyes of the government, and bury some skeletons that were still knocking loudly from within my closet.

Christine didn't really understand why I had such a look of wonder and amazement in my eyes, but she let me keep the newspaper when she was done. Within it, I found the name of the Hungarian translator in the article and decided to call him the next morning.

We arranged to meet at a coffee shop before my shift that day. I wasted no time and quickly but cordially asked him if he could introduce me to the Lion King who was involved with the story. Before a waitress could have checked on us, he made a phone call to the Lion King and within five minutes had me an appointment with him that evening at the 52nd division of the Royal Canadian Mounted Police in midtown Toronto.

Ever since my incident with the Hungarian customs officers, I was nervous around any type of authority. However, I had faith that the Canadian police would behave differently from the Hungarians. Also, having a translator along gave me an extra boost of confidence. We walked into the station and I was greeted by Detective White and Detective Morgan at the front desk. Detective White was leading the investigation I had read about, and Detective Morgan was his partner.

We moved promptly into the guts of the station, winding down sterile hallways to an interview room stocked with a waiting video camera and four chairs.

As we sat down, I noticed that Morgan was the younger of the two detectives. White's hair was speckled with salt and pepper. Both looked really friendly, and seemed very at home throughout the process.

"Now Timea," White started. "Why don't you tell us why you're here?"

"Well, it's a long story" I said to my translator, who then repeated my phrases to the officers in English. "And some of it may be hard to believe. I have been called a liar by the police in Hungary and I sincerely hope that you'll trust me."

"Well, you may as well try," they said in unison, and I began.

Throughout everything, Morgan constantly asked me how I was feeling, if I was okay or needed water; and after eight hours of recorded testimony, the detectives offered to drive me home.

On the way home, the translator explained that the police had decided to press charges against Alfonzo, the owner of the first club I worked for. They would move in to make the arrest when they got a few more pieces of evidence to support my testimony. They explained that if they managed to press charges against him, I would have to testify in court. But because of my illegal status, they would need to keep me in the country until the case could be brought before a judge. After that, I was on my own and would either have to leave or put in an application for refugee status. The translator said that he had worked on a lot of refugee cases in the past and that he believed my case to be a solid one. It was a cold evening in the middle of a

Canadian winter when the three men wished me well. I shut the cruiser door, making my way alone through the front door of my townhouse.

I went upstairs, but I was too spun to get any sleep. I could barely think. I'd spilled the beans! I needed the sun to come up so I chain-smoked cigarettes in hopes of coaxing it out. Shortly thereafter, I received a call from Detective Morgan in the afternoon. He sounded lively and offered to introduce me to a social worker in the Annex. "It's a young area of Toronto that's littered with book stores, coffee shops and breakfast joints. You'll love it" he informed me casually. I didn't need much convincing. I yearned to talk without fear to someone (anyone) without judgment or prejudice. Morgan said the social worker's name was Jeff and that he'd take me whenever I was ready. Before the phone call was over, we had a date.

Walking briskly downtown, I was guided into a high paced area of Toronto. I was anxious to get in out of the cold when Morgan led me into a very old Victorian building that was clearly a social agency. I learned later that this agency worked with sex workers who wanted to get away from the business. They offered counseling, medical referrals, and many other services for people in need. It seemed we had an appointment and went straight into Jeff's office.

Instantly approachable, warm and smiling broadly, Jeff offered me his hand. He was in his mid-thirties, African-Canadian, and showed me the utmost respect. We didn't really talk about everything that I felt I 'had' to tell the police. Instead we simply shot the breeze. Our topics ranged from English language practice to hobbies, the weather in Hungary, and finally, a small confession about my desire for a real job completely outside the illegal or immoral crowd. I loved everything that Alex had done for me at the club but needed to think about how to sustain myself in Canada for the long term, and I yearned to disassociate from the trade.

"If you took a walk down Bloor, you'd be surprised at the number of places hiring," Jeff said coaxingly. "They don't care how much English you speak, as long as you can make a good coffee."

"I'm not sure that I can." I replied.

"Well, what did you do in Hungary before you came here? Do you have a resume or anything?" he asked.

"A what?" I responded.

"A resume - it tells people what kind of work you've done in the past." I must have looked confused because Jeff went on. "It's a personalized document that demonstrates to an employer whether or not someone is a good candidate for a job."

"But I've only worked on a Hungarian television show and served alcohol in a strip club," I wondered out loud. "Who would hire me?"

"Hey you're here talking to me, and that shows that you're taking responsibility. Give yourself a little bit of credit," he said with a smile. I knew that he was right. I looked outside and saw that the sun was shining. When our conversation was over, I decided not to waste the day, and instead, I took a walk around some uncharted territory.

Out of the building and off the main streets, I made my way into a small bouncing arts district. I was smiling as I walked past creamy smelling cheese shops, art supply stores, eccentric video shops and buzzing coffee shops packed with fashionable students. I stopped at a popular bakery that seemed instantly to stay with you. It was hard to explain, but just being around the aesthetic of the bakery seemed to enhance my well-being that day. They had a live string band playing, massive cookies in the window, potted plants hanging from the ceiling and pierced cashiers serving bagels with cream cheese. My senses were shorting out and the sun just kept on shining.

The street was very slowly paced and mostly pedestrian. Strolling casually across it, I saw a second story hair salon and decided to see if they were hiring. I don't quite know what I was thinking at that moment, but I was so completely charged with confidence that frankly, I didn't care if they laughed me out onto the street and back to Hungary. I was on top of the world and wholly surprised to open the door to face an Eastern European woman at the front desk.

"Hi!" She greeted me in a strong accent. "How can I help you?" I was thrown off, but told her that I was looking for a job. "Oh, you're a hairdresser?"

I shook my head, "Not officially, but I could clean and wash hair, sweep the floors you know, that kind of thing."

"Well, my name is Panni. Where did you come from?"

"I'm Hungarian originally," I said, and quickly clarified, "but this is my home now."

She excused herself to take a phone call and a lump swelled up in the back of my throat. What was I doing here? I looked around for a way to escape my brash stupidity. This place had such an identity. I could never fit in at a place like this, showing up with a coffee in the morning, my hair looking healthy and no bags under my eyes. "Sorry about that," she said, looking me in the eyes. "It may just be your lucky day. Now I'm not the owner but I've heard talk around the shop about finding another girl to pick up the phones and mind the washing and sweeping duties."

"My English is good enough for answering the phones? You really think so?" I asked.

She gave me a smile, "There's always someone else in the shop if you're in a jam. Don't worry about a thing - just a second, dear."

She hopped up and walked into the back room, pushing a curtain out of her way as she disappeared. I was so scared. All I knew was how to serve alcohol in a strip joint. What did I know about customer service? As fast as she left, the woman came back with another more petite woman a footstep behind her. The smaller woman was wearing dark glasses inside the bright salon and had slivers of hair that matched her bright purple summer dress. "My name is Eve. I hear that you're looking for a job." This accent I knew. She was at least raised in England and felt like a comfortable blend of both 'in' and 'nowhere near' her element. I nodded excitedly.

"Do you have a SIN card?" she asked.

"No," I answered honestly.

"Ever um, worked in a salon before?"

"No," I answered again.

"Are you allowed to work in Canada, hun?"

"No," I replied, again.

"Well, that wasn't so bad", I thought. "It could have been worse". Amazingly, she continued. "What are your hobbies?" She hadn't yet looked away and still seemed excited. "You enjoy doing your own hair in the morning?"

"Yes, actually I had a small television show in Hungary," I went on "and I didn't even need a stylist," I added. She was smiling and standing closer to me now. She looked to be about six feet tall.

"Let me introduce you to my partner," and she turned away, shouting over her shoulder, "You'll like her!"

Marianne came out with incredible speed. Surging with an almost visible energy, she fixed her square glasses and shook my hand. The three women looked at me with smiles on their faces. "My name's Timea," I said. "It's nice to meet you all."

Chapter 14

Eve and Marianne were waiting for an answer and apparently I hadn't said a word. Eve looked at me playfully, "Hello? Is that a yes?" she asked. "Tomorrow?

Oh yes, I'd love to. What time?" I finally responded.

"Nine sharp and don't be late now!" was her enthusiastic reply.

We all shook hands and from that point on, my feet never touched the ground. With each step down the stairs to the bustling street, my gaze shifted from one part of the neighborhood to the next, observing everything that I could and grinning in disbelief. For the next few weeks I'd survive on three hours of sleep per night. I worked both jobs, from 9 a.m. to 7 p.m. at the salon and 7 p.m. to 4 a.m. behind the bar. At first glance, one could rightfully assume that I would be a tired sack of lifelessness, but on the contrary, the charged atmosphere of the salon had me out of bed faster then an IV bag chocked full of fine ground espresso.

Everything at the salon was new and exciting to me, including getting soaked to the elbows after my first shampoo and drenching clients by mistake. Eve and Marianne stood behind me throughout all the initial bobbles and foibles while I got a handle on the pace of the shop. To say it was a welcome change would be an understatement. I was introduced to every client by name (I was still going by

Alysson) and was encouraged to think of the shop as my home and to treat the guests as friends.

When asked what I was doing alone in Canada, it hurt me, but I had to lie. I said that I had come as a nanny and loved it too much to go home after my contract was finished. I couldn't tell my new friends about my past and opted for some noble fibs instead. Even recalling the memories, let alone formulating them into words, felt inappropriate in this relaxing environment. Jazz from the 40's was played around the clock and original ceramic work made by Eve and Marianne lined the walls and housed the lush plants that hung from the ceiling on thin brass chains. Behind the plants the walls were lined with cubist paintings. The sun shone bright inside the building and everyone brimmed with stories about the area. The shop had been there for twenty years and they had clients who had been returning since they had opened.

Even though it was my primary income, I had to cut down my hours at the club and I decided to bartend strictly on weekends. I was waiting to hear back from the detectives who were in the midst of collecting evidence against Alfonzo when one day I got a call from Detective Morgan.

"Are you free tomorrow, Timea?" he asked. "Immigration would like to hear your story first hand."

I was scared. The Hungarian chauffeurs had told us horror stories about Immigration officers and I had first hand experience of what they were capable of in Hungary. They were incredibly powerful and I imagined that they didn't care if you were killed in a cell by an officer or another foreigner. One less illegal meant one less illegal immigrant's paper work for them to do. "I'll have to tell the girls at the salon and take a day off," I replied.

"No problem," he said. "I'll call you tonight to confirm and see you tomorrow bright and early."

I didn't sleep that night. Transitioning between fits of fearful tears and sharp pains in my stomach I wished I could call Eve or Marianne and tell them everything that had happened to me. I felt sick. Would these life altering traumas ever cease? Could I truly live a normal life or was I destined to bear this weight alone forever?

When I woke up the next morning and looked into the mirror, I could have sworn I'd skipped my twenties and found middle age before my time. My eyes were heavy, my spirit restless and crows feet were sliding sharply towards my temples. Examining my complexion closely, I leapt off the ground as the phone rang. Detective Morgan said he was downstairs. As I sat quietly in his car, he explained I would be interviewed by two Immigration officers and that the RCMP would also be present taking notes. He put it calmly, but it felt like I was en route to my own execution. He told me I had to tell the truth no matter what. And that once the interview was done, officers would review my statements and decide if I would be allowed to stay in Canada during the case or be deported instead.

After a long drive, we pulled up in front of the curb of a large building. It was overflowing with people and families standing in a line with their belongings in bags and looking at their shoes. They were awaiting deportation. We walked into a large interview room to find five people waiting. Two officers from the RCMP, Detective Morgan's partner, and two immigration officers were present. The immigration officers started the conversation.

The first officer was tough. A female who showed no sympathy, she grilled me while her male partner remained quiet. The rest of the room took notes. I started to break down in only minutes. I wanted to cry. I fought it. The way she asked her questions made me think that she didn't believe a word I said. No matter what answer I gave her, it wasn't good enough. I looked to Detective Morgan for support, but he couldn't interrupt. I excused myself to the restroom and after having a good cry, I collected myself. Refreshing my face in the mirror I watched the tears mingle with splashed water on the sink. I dried it all off, took a deep breath and returned.

The interview finally concluded after a couple of long and difficult hours. I later learned that the tactics used by Immigration were designed to break the subject down.
If the subject could withstand the relentless questioning and continue coming up with the same story, then it was deemed likely that they were telling the truth. While it was incredibly difficult, I knew they were just doing their job. They had to be convinced that I wasn't creating a story just so they'd let me stay in the country. To this day, I have random flashbacks from that interview.

After the ordeal, Detective Morgan, the younger male immigration officer and I went outside for a smoke. As they were talking shop, I looked into this young man's eyes to see if I could tell which way he was leaning. Would he allow me to stay or send me away? His name was Officer Massimo and he seemed wise beyond his years. I could tell he enjoyed his work as he and Detective Morgan spoke and I wondered if he had any idea that the decision he was about to make could either save my life or put me in serious danger. How many times a day did he make similarly life-changing decisions for other individuals? We finished our cigarettes and I took one last long look at him.

On the way home, Detective Morgan told me that as painful as it was, it was their job to make sure they had the proper description of what happened. He said that if they decided to press charges against Alfonzo for sexual assault, I'd probably stay for the proceedings.

He knew I was still working part time at the Red Rose, so he told me to be careful and quit soon if I could. I thought he was just being considerate, but I'd soon find out why he gave me the heads up. Detective Morgan called to tell me Immigration had made a decision and we needed to go back to the building where I had my questioning.

"Do I need to pack my belongings?" I managed to ask with some restraint.

"No, Timea. You don't have to pack." he responded.

I hung up the phone and looked towards the sky in a state of blissful gratitude. But how were they going to arrest Alfonzo? Was I safe with the case proceeding? Should I quit my job? How would I pay the rent? How long would the court case go on? Would I have to appear? I was quiet as Detective Morgan once again drove me to Immigration. "Don't worry, Timea. It's just going to be us and Officer Massimo. No one else will be there and there won't be any more interrogating. We just need to complete some paperwork." As promised, a much more comfortable looking Officer Massimo met us inside.

He took my photo, fingerprints, and other information to issue the Temporary Work Permit that would be effective for one year. He also asked for my passport, saying he had to hold it in his office as long as I was in Canada. That was my only identification so surrendering it was difficult. Massimo informed me that I was to call him every time I changed my address or phone number as Immigration now had to know of my whereabouts at all times. Once we wrapped up, Detectives Morgan and Massimo and I went outside for a smoke. As I stood there watching them talk, I remembered standing in exactly the same spot a few weeks earlier. I remembered how different my heart rate was then.

Officer Massimo courteously handed me his business card and said, "If you have any problems or questions, please don't hesitate to get in touch." I looked at the card and found the sense of comfort that I derived from it ironic, considering how my former captors had portrayed Canadian immigration officers. How entirely different they were in reality. I never saw it coming. We finished our cigarettes and said our goodbyes.

Chapter 15

I was still working part time at the Red Rose Club and six days a week at the salon. As I became more accustomed to a 'normal' environment, working at the strip club became a real effort. That being said, I needed the extra cash because minimum wage in Toronto wasn't cutting it. Christmas rolled around and since it wasn't much of a holiday for me, I worked while my family was home in Hungary putting up a tree and wrapping gifts. Calling home was difficult, just hearing their voices made me sad. I was homesick and they were worried about me.

Their suspicions about my well-being grew when my mom received a call from a strange man saying her daughter owed him a lot of money and that she was safe as long as she wasn't in Hungary. When she told me about the conversation, I lied. I said it must have been a mistake. I had become good at avoiding the subject so the questions stopped. Our conversations remained light and superficial.

One February afternoon, I arrived early for my shift at the Red Rose and was talking on the pay phone near the front door when hell broke loose. The door beside me was being kicked in by cops who came crashing in like a stampede. I looked up to see police officers piling in and barking orders. "It's a raid! Turn the lights off! Nobody move!"

I froze. As I watched the uniformed officers run past, one caught my eye. Then others started to look familiar. It was

Detective White, the lead investigator in Project Almonzo and just behind him were Detectives Morgan, Jeff and Officer Massimo.

What was I supposed to do? Should I pretend I didn't know them? I stood by the payphone waiting for a signal. The music stopped and the house lights came on. Surprised, the waitresses and bartenders stood around. Detective White came toward me and winked, saying loudly,

"Miss, you by the phone, please step inside and take a seat."

He was very firm but the wink let me know I needed to play along. They pulled Alex from his office and told him to stay put. Some of the officers ran upstairs and came down with boxes while others interviewed the dancers and staff. Detective Morgan was interviewing the DJ while Office Massimo was checking IDs and work permits.

"Who's responsible for the bar and the cash?" asked Detective White.

"That would be me, sir," I replied.

"I need you to open the register and sit down in that corner until someone comes to talk to you. And don't touch anything," he added. I opened the register and sat down where he told me, far enough away that no one could hear my conversation with the officers.

Once out of sight from the rest of the staff, Officer Massimo came over to me. Detective Morgan joined him. "I'm so sorry about this, Timea. Are you okay?" he asked.

"Yes, thank you," I replied. "I'll call you about this tomorrow," he said.

Detective White quickly sidled in, "Don't worry. I don't need to know how much money is in the register, but please keep counting and write it down. I just wanted you away from everyone else. We're going to take your papers like we're doing for everyone but we'll give them back to you. Do you understand?" he asked.

"I do. Thank you, Detective."

After completing the interviews an hour later, officers escorted two girls and Alex out of the building in handcuffs. I didn't know why they arrested Alex, but since I had come to know and trust these officers, I knew there must have been a good reason. But I was rattled by the experience. Because I was familiar with some of the officers, it was a surreal experience. My emotions were all over the place. I felt badly for Alex and the staff, and Iwas embarrassed knowing that now Detectives Morgan, White, Officer Massimo and Jeff all knew that I still worked at the Red Rose. Detective Morgan phoned the next day to apologize for not being able to warn me about the raid. He said twelve undercover agents had been inside investigating illegal sexual and drug-related activities. It was all very overwhelming and felt like a scene from a movie I had not agreed to be in.

Detective Morgan phoned a few weeks later to let me know that the police had raided the Pink Dolls Club and arrested Alfonzo in the process. He appeared in handcuffs in the newspaper the following day. The article stated there was evidence Alfonzo sexually assaulted a young woman from Hungary, and the court date was pending. Detective Morgan went on to say that they had found a copy of my passport and work permit at his house when it was searched. Of course, Alfonzo denied all charges, but I felt safe knowing Jeff, Detective Morgan and Officer Massimo were only a phone call away if Alfonzo tried to find me.

I needed to keep a lower profile in light of the pending case, so I quit my job at the Red Rose immediately. It would take a year before Alfonzo's case would come to trial. The thought of waiting an entire year to testify against him in court was daunting at best, and I became terrified at the thought of him sitting, listening to me talk before a full courtroom about what he had done to me. At least I was allowed to stay in Canada for another year while I waited to testify.

With some time to reflect, I thought about all of the people along the way who had helped me, in particular Detective Morgan, Officer Massimo and Jeff - my three guardian angels. I was finally able to breathe, knowing I was safe for the time being. I rented a one bedroom apartment in a beautiful area that reminded me of the nicer side of Budapest. It was called Forest Hill. The rolling terrain housed lovely homes and reminded me of the part of my hometown that looked down over the Danube.

With my Sundays now free, I offered to help clean Eve and Marianne's house to keep my mind occupied. The fact was that I didn't have any family or friends around so going to their house was a pleasure. It was a very inviting place with a gorgeous backyard and luscious garden. The art studio was always humming with some new project. The meals were delicious, and their four cats became great companions. These two women nursed and nurtured my soul.

One Sunday afternoon as I walked down on a street near my apartment, I stumbled upon a cute little ceramics store where you could make and paint your own pottery pieces. I knew right away the two gifts I wanted to make. Since Detective Morgan and Officer Massimo drank a lot of coffee, mugs would be just the thing. I personalized each and was touched by how thankful they were.

Working for Eve and Marianne over the next year, I slowly started to make friends and build a life for myself. I still avoided deep, intimate connections however, because I knew my time in Canada was limited.

Just weeks before the court proceedings were set to begin, Alfonzo came down with medical problems, delaying the procedures yet another year. Two years turned into four. Four years turned into six. Still unable to leave the country, but fortunate enough to have a legal work permit, I was beginning to lose faith that the case would ever come to trial.

For another two years, I continued to work for Eve and Marianne, but eventually found other bartending and waitressing positions in Toronto. I even got a new cat of my own. His name is Massimo. He's now nine years old and remains a great love in my life.

Over the next several years, I tried to find a position in the film and television industry, but no one would hire me because I didn't have the proper credentials. I also wanted to work with children because of my strong initial interest in school, but again, no one would hire me. I didn't have the advanced educational background and my temporary work permit didn't allow me to continue my education. It looked as though I'd be serving drinks and food for at least a little while longer.

Having vowed to prove to Officer Massimo and Detective Morgan that they made the right decision, advocating for me to stay in Canada, I dreamed I'd one day make them proud. I also wanted to pay my respects to a country that was essentially a surrogate mother. Not only did Canada afford me a life free from further exploitation, it gave me a place to call home and a brand new beginning.

My biological mother finally came to Canada for a visit in 2000. Her career had been in law enforcement so Detective Morgan gave her and me the grand tour of police headquarters along with a personal trip to the breathtaking wonder that is Niagara Falls. I knew I didn't want to return to Hungary, so as the court date extensions kept coming, I toyed with the idea of applying for permanent Canadian status versus going to England and once again, starting all over. Not having any family in Canada was, and is to this day like missing a limb.

At twenty-six years old with no 'formal' education, I was well aware that my experience in the past gave me a mandate to share my story with more people than those whom I could reach in the restaurant business as a waitress. I developed a passion for non-profit organizations and found that I gravitated towards volunteering. I started out volunteering for a crisis hotline and I was fortunate enough to receive training in crisis and trauma counseling. It dawned on me that I was able to connect with, understand and support people in unfortunate and difficult situations.

The court date rolled around, but by this time I'd become a different person. I no longer felt like a victim or felt threatened by Alfonzo. I wasn't afraid to go to court either. I was ready and I looked forward to putting the past behind me.

Chapter 16

The long-awaited day in court arrived, and Alfonzo's defense attorney tore me to shreds. However, there were times during the three-hour cross examination when I stopped him dead in his tracks. I recalled everything that had happened as truthfully as I could remember while looking directly at Alfonzo. Sitting directly behind him was Alfonzo's brother. He mocked me. Raising his hands to his throat and bringing them down like an axe.

"Did anyone see that?" I said, stopping mid-sentence. "That man is gesturing that he's going to cut my throat."

I was more amused than scared. After all I had been through, it would take a lot more than that to frighten me. Thankfully, the Judge ordered him to leave the courtroom. When the trial ended, Alfonzo's ruthless defense attorney shook my hand and said, "I just want to wish you the best of luck. You're by far the toughest witness I've ever dealt with. I hope you'll be able to put this behind you." He knew Alfonzo was guilty, but he was getting paid to do a job. I remember his words and face to this day. He repeatedly called me a liar with a wild imagination and then had the nerve to extend his hand in best wishes once the gavel fell. Lawyers can have the most malleable personalities sometimes. Perhaps it's what they get paid for.

Throughout the turbulent weeks surrounding the trial, I was living with my boyfriend Wayne whom I met working at a Toronto theme restaurant called Medieval Times. It was a tense time for us as my court appearance had me on edge. Although we had some arguments, they weren't particularly serious. I edited what I told him about my past, thinking he couldn't handle it, and frankly, I didn't want him to know the details. This was my chance to start over, too.

A few weeks before I was scheduled to appear in court, Wayne started having nasty anxiety attacks which quickly escalated into full fledged breakdowns. Just a week after my court appearance, I got an unnerving call from him and raced home to find him white as a ghost, shaking and making no sense. I asked him to go to the doctor, but he refused. The phone rang. It was a relief to hear Detective Morgan's voice on the other end. He called to say they had finally reached a verdict in Alfonzo's case. Not guilty on all charges. I couldn't react. "Hello? Timea?" Detective Morgan said. I could only feel the phone in the palm of my hand, nothing else. "Timea, are you there?"

I stared at the wall paper beside the telephone.

"Timea you did everything you could do. Timea?" In my periphery, Wayne shut the bathroom door and I jolted upright. "Are you there?" he asked.

"Yes, sorry." I finally answered.

"Timea, you did everything you could. You were brave. Time wasn't on our side. I hope you can put this behind you and press on. Please make sure you put in your application for your status. You have my phone number, so call me from time to time so that I know how you're doing."

I could tell by the tone of his voice he felt badly for me and wished there was something more he could have done. It was a very late Friday night and I was still at work when Wayne called. Still trying to recover from my conversation with Detective Morgan, I had to snap back to reality when I realized Wayne was accusing me of cheating on him. He wasn't himself and I tried in vain to calm him down.

Emotionally exhausted, I told Wayne that I had to work late, and since we lived an hour and a half away from the office where I worked at the time, I'd stay at a friend's house for the evening. I had to work again early the next morning and was too worn out to make the drive home safely.

I arrived at my friend's house, and called home. I told Wayne I didn't have the strength to fight and that we could go out for lunch and a walk when I got home the following evening. We said goodnight and I tried to go to sleep, but my mind wouldn't allow it.

What could I have done or said differently during my testimony? Will I ever see or talk to Detective Morgan again? Since my status was ending, would that mean my friendship with Officer Massimo would be over too?

These two men knew me better than anyone else in my new circle of friends, and the thought of losing them added insult to the injury of Alfonzo's verdict. Sleep never came.

I thought a lot about the court case and Alfonzo. Life had been difficult for him over the past six years. Not only did he have to report to the police station every Tuesday, he couldn't go near a club and he couldn't leave the country. So in my own small way I decided he had served some time. He was inconvenienced for six years, and I suppose

I'm glad he didn't end up in jail. In spite of everything, I don't think I could live with the thought that someone went to jail on my behalf. It was much easier to try to forgive than to live with guilt hanging over me.

I called Wayne the following morning to check in and was surprised when he didn't answer the phone. I was anxious to see him and explain what had happened with Alfonzo's case, so I was pleased to have a smooth drive home, completely devoid of traffic. My cat Massimo and Wayne's cat both greeted me anxiously as I opened the door. I called for Wayne but he didn't answer. I walked toward the bathroom near the back of the apartment and Massimo playfully pawed at my feet. He had never done that before.

Again I called for Wayne and again my own voice echoed about the apartment. I went to the living room, and I saw he had taken a nap earlier because the blanket was on the couch, his morning coffee cup remained on the coffee table. I walked towards the back of the apartment and saw towels all over the floor. *That's odd; I thought why would he leave towels on the floor?* As I peered into my room, I noticed the bookcase was pulled off the wall and a long TV cable was hanging out, disconnected. There was still no sign of Wayne. I called again. *Was he fixing something again?* He was a genius when it came to problem solving and handy work. I headed towards the laundry room thinking he might be in there when I turned and saw what Massimo had been pawing about. Wayne was in the bathroom. I froze, took a deep breath and slowly tilted my head to take in the off-kilter, inhuman way he was swaying back and forth. He was gone. And he had been gone for hours.

I felt a weird, cold sensation coming through the top of my head like a local anesthetic. Everything was blurry and my watch stopped. I somehow managed to get to the living room. I picked up the phone and walked outside. It was March 13, 2004. 7:08pm. I sat outside on the curb wearing no jacket or shoes and dialed 911 in the cold. When the operator picked up I could only utter the basics. "My boyfriend just committed suicide" I said.

I proceeded to hit 'rock bottom.' No one should have to grieve alone, but that is exactly what I was doing. I attempted to rebuild myself without any family or close friends to support me but remained grief stricken and unable to work or even function.

I wasn't prepared for the aftermath of Wayne's death. I realized the past six years weren't as bad as they could have been, when Wayne's parents locked me out of the apartment and took everything I owned. They forced me to fight for my very own cat and left me without a thing. Aside from one pair of pants, a pair of socks, a T-shirt and my cat, everything I had was gone. Spring found me living in a shelter.

Writing in my journal I looked around the room for what seemed like days and days. I lost track of how many nights I cried until my tears turned to dust. I sat like a statue, unable to flinch. No one could shake me out of my stupor. Sad families, teenage girls in used clothes, putrid smelling abusers with rancid hygiene all danced around me like ghosts in the wind. And it was in this moment of complete abject stupefaction that I realized that I couldn't relate to my environment or those in it any longer. I had no choice but to take responsibility for myself and move on. This was my moment of clarity.

Chapter 17

It is October 6th, 2009. I am sitting in a large venue awaiting my turn to speak at the International Sex Crimes Seminar for Police in the Greater Toronto Area. I am the featured guest speaker on the topic of human trafficking. With approximately five hundred officers in the audience, my eyes are peeling across the room, looking for two in particular.

I hear my name. The crowd welcomes me with applause, and nervously I make it to the podium. As I'm introducing myself I suddenly spot Detective Morgan and Officer Massimo sitting in the back of the room smiling proudly. I stand up tall, give a subtle wave, and start my speech.

"Hello everyone, my name is Timea E. Nagy and my story begins in 1998. Shortly after answering an ad in Budapest, Hungary…"

Author's Reflection - Choices

You can be raised in poverty, you can be raised in a wealthy family, and you can grow up in a foster home or in a different country. But at the end of the day, your childhood does define who you are, right? Wrong. You can live your adult life as a reflection of what you were taught as a child but once you grow up you have any number of opportunities to take another look at yourself. If any of those values don't resonate with you then you have the power to construct a new belief system for yourself.

You can choose to be angry with your parents for the rest of your life and judge them until they pass away, or you can choose to realize that they weren't perfect, and move on. We are all human beings who are fighting our own fight, and sometimes frustration and anxiety can make people do regretful, harmful things. I chose to blame a lot of things on my mother, father, brother, and the way I grew up. I chose to believe that I had it bad and often asked the question, "why me?" I grew up in Budapest, Hungary in the 1970's where things were a lot different.

Back then, domestic violence was normal, alcoholism was ubiquitous and working for the government was the only rewarding thing you could do. I grew up in a poor household and my parents divorced when I was nine. I had an older brother, who took his anger out on me day after day. I had no one to talk to. I had nowhere to go when I was scared. Many evenings my parents screamed and yelled at each other and at times my Dad would choke my mother until she was blue. Sometimes my Mom would pick fights with him as he drank.

Our apartment was small and I always dreamt of living in a beautiful home. I was too embarrassed to bring anyone home to play, and many nights my brother and I were left alone at home. My Dad wasn't around and he remained vacant when he was. My Mom worked seventeen hours a day so that we could pay the bills. One Christmas Eve they turned off our electricity because my Dad drank away the money that was saved for the bill.

One night my brother and I woke up to realize that my mom was hanging out the window, threatening to jump. We lived on the third floor and the whole neighbourhood saw it: classmates, some of our teachers. Imagine going to school the next day and trying to act normal.

Another Christmas Eve, my mom, brother and I were living in the master bedroom. My dad lived in the small room across the hall because my parents were separated at the time. My Mom locked us in with her and refused to let my dad in. He got drunk and started to yell from beyond the glass door. It doesn't take much provocation to make a drunken man violent. My dad broke the glass and we ran outside. Barefooted and jacket-less we ran through the broken glass and snow. We ran down the street and my mom took us to a neighbour's house where she called the police.

My brother had to find a way to cope, so he picked on me all the time. Or, he'd go to soccer games and later he became a fanatic. He'd find a way to let out his anger after every single game. He used to chase other fans and get into fights. They called him Bull. He was a very angry child who used to set fire to my fish and torture my only friend, a stuffed animal. I was scared all of the time because whenever I went home from school, I never knew what I was going home to.

Is it horrific? It was for me. Was I scared? Of course. Did I have any choice? As a child, not really. So how did I get through all of this? I took art classes and I volunteered at the local library after school. I created clubs myself. I recruited class members to go and visit elderly people in the senior home not far from our school. I was on the basketball team and in the chorus as a soprano. I wrote for the school paper. I organized school trips. I created a fan club for a famous Hungarian singer. I did anything to keep me away from home.

When we played tournaments, everyone's parents were there, sitting proudly in the crowd. I was too embarrassed to tell my dad to come because of his bad reputation. My mom was working all the time, so she couldn't attend. This was my childhood in a nutshell. I can sit here and think of millions of people who had it worse than I did. And I can sit here and think of another million who had amazing childhoods and became tortured alcoholics and abusive self destroyers on their own, independent of the privileged childhood they were blessed with.

They all made choices in their lives.

Instinct and Choices

There is a guiding system inside each of us. It's amazing. You know what I'm talking about. I know you've felt it during times of immediate decision. Well, what I learned about my own instinct, was that feeling in your stomach, that shakiness or queasiness, different for everyone, had never let me down.

Did I always listen? Of course not. After making a wrong decision, my instinct pestered me persistently. The decision I made when I came to Canada was the most outstanding that I can remember. But let me tell you, did I know that something was 'off' with the job offer and the agency? Yes. Deep inside I knew something was weird. I didn't listen to my instinct. I went against it and I lost.

But hold on a second. I have endured horrible experiences and I didn't listen to the signs. Some people say that I deserved what I got (however I don't think anyone deserves to suffer.) But would I do it all over again? Absolutely! I feel like I learned so much, so quickly about people and human nature. More than my age's worth, that's for sure.

Knowing what I know today, at the age of 32, I can say that I am listening to my instincts. I only allow experiences into my life if I know that I will personally grow from them. I know that I am strong enough to handle whatever life throws at me because of my instinct. We may not have control over every event that occurs to us, but we do have control over our choices and responses to these events.

We may not have control over losing a loved one, or watching someone die from a long wasting illness, but we do have control over how we handle it. We can handle it with grace. We can find a way to cope in a way that will benefit us and with luck, maybe others too.

My decision to go to Canada came at a crucial time for me and my brother. We were living in an apartment. My mom moved out to try a new life with her long, lost love from twenty five years earlier. We were in our early twenties and we were really happy for her, but it was a far-fetched thought that we could manage a household and be responsible on our own.

I created a small production company with two other young guys. We did music videos and concert films for up and coming stars. The money was great when we had a gig. But for the four months prior to my trip to Canada, we had no money coming in and things were going downhill pretty fast. My brother and I were almost evicted. We had to come up with a lot of money to cover our mortgage for the prior six months. I was desperate to find a job that would help us to get out of debt and save our home. My instinct was right there to protect me and warned me about that next step I took, namely leaving the place that I was trying to save, but I didn't listen. Even now, almost a decade later, I still remember what it felt like.

One thing I've learned is that my gut feeling will always be there for me but the decision to heed it or ignore it is mine alone. I made a conscious choice to come to Canada and try to do whatever I could to save our house. I knew I put myself in a very dangerous situation, but I thought that regardless of the danger, I'd eventually come home in one piece, save the house and pay the bills.

I made one bad choice and I have lived with the guilt stemming from it for the last ten years. I hid from my old friends and family because I felt guilty. I hid in a country far away from my home, and I tried to escape my own reality. I was trying to hide who I was in my past, and what had happened to me. It wasn't working. It was then that I made a choice to make my life better. I made a choice to get rid of the guilt that wouldn't let me be who I am today because I was afraid that people would judge me, and say that it was my own fault.

As I wrote this book, I eventually realized that the most vocal critic of myself had been staring back at me in front of the mirror for all these years. From that moment on, I made a choice to live my life guilt free.

Any of my readers who have lived with guilt know what I am describing. How long has it been? Ten, twenty, thirty years? Have you been keeping it a secret? Your father raped you, or your mother abused you. The neighbour touched you, your teacher bothered you, your brother, your sister, your uncle, your friend, your relative was inappropriate with you.

No matter what happened to you or who did it to you, or whatever caused the tremendous amount of guilt that has lead you to an addiction or instability in your life, you know what I am talking about. No matter what happened to you, you can make the choice to look into the mirror and face your demons! Get support, get counselling, and make sure you have someone you can trust throughout this process. But make the first step because believe me, speaking your own truth to another is priceless and liberating.

Speaking your truth will give you your freedom back. Speaking your truth will inspire others, empower you and set you free. Trust me on this one, I speak from experience.

Special Thanks

I don't really know where to start or where to finish with my thanks, so many hands have helped me along the way, but I will try.

Thanks to my mom, my brother, my step dad, my dad, my step sister, my "adopted sister" for all of their support.

Thanks to my mentor, spiritual teacher, and dear friend **Claudia Brazil** for opening my eyes so that I could recognize my destiny. Thank you Mike Yosher, for letting me heal, grow and making me feel safe and loved.

Special thanks from the bottom of my heart to TPS, Sergeant **Michael Josifovic**, and TPS, Det.Cst, **Mario Catenaccio.**

Mike: Thank you for taking my calls at 2 am. Thank you for taking me to the hospital when I had no one to call. Thank you for giving my dignity back. Thank you for teaching me how to drink Tim Hortons and not burn my hand. Thank you for changing my beliefs about the law enforcement. You are always going to be the #1 Detective.

Mario: Thank you for standing up for me and making it possible for me to stay in this country. Your action saved my life. Thank you for sharing your wisdom, thank you for staying in touch with me throughout the years, and always looking out for me. And thank you for everything you taught me. Without your help I would not be here today alive.

For the last 12 years, anything I have done, I have done it because I wanted to prove it to both of you that I was worth saving. You were my motivation and inspiration. Thank you.

David Cormican, Dr. Rob H., Jayme L., Sarah B. and Jessica F. - thank you for being there for me when I really needed a friend.

Thank you to all my friends in Canada and the few friends I have left in Hungary.

A huge special thanks to my new friend and soul brother, Colum Begley. Without you Colum, this book would never have come to life.

And thanks to everyone who helped me grow, support, learn and just get through the tough times:

Jeff Lanza and his beautiful family, Gyovai Eva, Fontanyi Zoltan, The Evanics Family, Nilu, Brenda, Charlene, Maurie C., and everyone at the RCMP Human Trafficking Coordination Center, Mrs. Joy Smith, Joel Oosterman Natasha Falle, Trisha Baptie, Forest, Mario, Members of the Toronto Police Services, The Vancouver Police Department Vice Unit, Edmonton Drugs and Vice Unit, The Peel Region Drugs and Vice Unit, Members of the OPP, York Regional Police and Drugs and Vice Unit, YRP Crime Stoppers, Mike Norman, Mike Viozzi, Scott, Heather, Thai T., Henry D., Dieter B., Ben Perrin, Tamara Cherry, Chief Armand, Bernice Carnegie, Brook Chambers, Rick Esther Bienstock, Marina Jemenez, Eve and Mariann, Mariah Udvardi, Shannon and Monica, Akos,

Pierrot, Arlene Y, Michael Cooper, Wayne Doucette, Rita Citron, Matt Kraus and the Kraus family, Julius Hegedus, Mark and Suzie and the Yosher family, Ben, Stefani Hartman, Dan Payne, Brenda Snow, Stacey Walsh, Christine Merritt and everyone at Medieval Times from 2000-2004, Yorkville Hair studio, James Joyce Irish Pub in the Annex, Blair Ohalaran, Loly Ricco, Lee and Story, Jenny Horsman, Nicole and Alex and the neighbors, Rosalie, Martha, Celeste, Rebeca, Sue, Chris, Patricia and Joe Elkerton, Thelma and Laney, Rob H, Joey Nativ, Jeremy E, Kate, Rabbia, Chauna, Leppa, Hussam, Tricia, Shannon and Monica, and God.

Suggested resources

Highly recommended!

1. **A book by Benjamin Perrin: Invisible chains**
   www.invisiblechains.ca
2. **SEX SLAVES Emmy award winner documentary by Ric Esther Bienstock,**
   www.pbs.org/wgbh/pages/frontline/slaves
3. **Buying Sex is Not a Sport**
   www.embracedignity.org
4. **Jessie Foster**
   www.jessiefoster.ca
5. **Walk With Me, Canadian Organization Helping Human Trafficked Victims**
   www.walk-with-me.org
6. **Not For Sale**
   www.notforsalecampaign.org

DNA, Demi and Ashton Foundation
http://demiandashton.org

freetheslaves.net
sharedhope.org
ecpat.net
humantrafficking.org
love146.org
unicef.org/protection
endhumantraffickingnow.com
castla.org
gems-girls.org
somaly.org
polarisproject.org

Glendene and Jessie Foster Award Ceremony, 2010
Det. Michael J. Morgan and Officer Mario C. Massimo receiving
an award from Timea Nagy for their compassion and dedication
to victims of human trafficking.

Mario Catenaccio ("Officer Massimo"), Me
and Michael Josifovic ("Det. Morgan").

Speaking at a Crime Stoppers Seminar, 2010

Timea Nagy and Retired FBI Special Agent Jeff Lanza,
following their presentation on human trafficking to a group
of Federal Judges in Kansas City, Missouri in March, 2010.

Mario the cat (Massimo)